Identifying
German Parian
Dolls

Identifying
GERMAN PARIAN
DOLLS

Mary Gorham Krombholz

This book is dedicated to
the countless Thuringian men, women and children who made
the antique dolls we collect and treasure today.

First edition/First printing

Copyright © 2006 Mary Gorham Krombholz. All rights reserved.
No part of the contents of this book may be reproduced without the
written permission of the publisher.

To purchase additional copies of this book, please contact:
Reverie Publishing Company, 130 South Wineow Street, Cumberland, MD 21502.
888-721-4999.
www.reveriepublishing.com

Library of Congress Control Number 2006923664
ISBN 1-932485-37-6

Project Editor: Krystyna Poray Goddu

Design: Jaye Medalia

Front and back cover photos: Estelle Johnston
Front cover, clockwise from top left:
Kling & Co, (see page 59), Alt Beck & Gottschalck (see page 42),
Alt Beck & Gottschalck (see page 46), Simon & Halbig (see page 107).
Back cover, clockwise from top left:
C.F. Kling & Co. (see page 62), Conta & Böhme (see page 98),
Simon & Halbig (see page109), Kestner & Co. (see page 127).

Photo page 2: Gregg Smith (see pages 8 and 9)

Printed and bound in Korea

Contents

PAGE 6   Foreword

PAGE 7   Introduction

PAGE 13   CHAPTER ONE: Porcelain Dollmaking in Germany

PAGE 24   The Porcelain Factories

PAGE 26   CHAPTER TWO: Alt, Beck & Gottschalck

PAGE 50   CHAPTER THREE: C. F. Kling & Co.

PAGE 78   CHAPTER FOUR: A.W. Fr. Kister

PAGE 86   CHAPTER FIVE: Conta & Böhme

PAGE 106   CHAPTER SIX: Simon & Halbig

PAGE 126   CHAPTER SEVEN: Kestner & Co.

PAGE 136   CHAPTER EIGHT: Hertwig & Co.

PAGE 152   Conclusion

PAGE 154   Glossary

PAGE 156   Bibliography

PAGE 159   Acknowledgments

Foreword

It is with great pride that I write this Foreword for Mary's fourth book, *Identifying German Parian Dolls*. I have been fortunate to accompany Mary in her quest for German-doll history for many years now, and I admire her enthusiasm and her wonderful ability to pick important facts about dollmakers out of reams and reams of material. It has always been important to Mary to share all her discoveries with the rest of the doll world, and that she has done amazingly well. This book will quench the thirst for help in identifying readers' own *Deutsche Puppensammlung* (German-Doll Collecting), all the time knowing that there will be more groundbreaking research from Mary.

With most great ideas, we all look back and say, "It's so simple! Why couldn't I have thought of that?" And so it is with Mary's approach to her research. You find the original porcelain factory, go to their dumping grounds to find their "seconds" tossed out a hundred years earlier, study the painting styles unique to that particular factory, and you're now able to identify the makers of unmarked dolls we've wondered about for years. Simple as that!

Of course, the key to all of this is Roland Schlegel, a walking encyclopedia of the German porcelain industry. While his intensive knowledge was instrumental in finding the locations of many long-forgotten factories, it is his ability to "charm the socks off" the elderly villagers that proved most useful. Older village residents, who were quite often former factory employees or sons or daughters of original factory workers, loved to reminisce about the good old days and then dig into their memories and recall the locations of dumping grounds of the various porcelain factories. That having been accomplished, Roland's job then was to watch over Mary and me on our treks to the dumping grounds, shovels in hand, to carry us over streams, to lift us onto platforms, to pull us up from stair-less basements—what fun! Once the digging began, Mary would draw out her Ziplock bags and carefully document the shards so everything would be in order once she was back at home and ready to begin her research.

While Mary's method of researching dollmakers is so logical, it is not an easy one. And now that most of the major old porcelain factories have been torn down and bulldozed over, it is not even possible any longer. Mary was in the right place at the right time with the right people. We are all benefiting from her years of hard work and painstaking documentation. This book is the result of her dedication for us to enjoy. Congratulations, Mary, on another job well done!

Your Dear Friend,
Susan Bickert, President, German Doll Company
July 2005

Introduction

Four parian-like shoulder heads, reflected in a mirror, are in the permanent collection of the doll museum in Sonneberg. This photograph was included in a group of slides offered for sale in the gift shop in the 1990s. The shoulder heads are, from left: two Simon & Halbig shoulder heads, an Alt, Beck & Gottschalck so-called Empress Eugenie shoulder head and a C.F. Kling & Co. shoulder head with an elaborately decorated shoulder plate.

The word parian is defined as fine, unglazed bisque that resembles the white marble found on the Greek island of Paros. Paros is one of the Cyclades island group located in the Aegean Sea southeast of Athens. Author Janet Johl provides the following information in her 1946 book *More About Dolls:* "The marble was hewn from the subterranean quarries of Paros for Praxiteles and his fellow sculptors. Thus, our Parian dolls of the 19th Century take us back to the 6th Century B.C., to the teeming life of one of the most artistic periods in human history."

Clara Fawcett provides an excellent definition of parian-like (which have often been called parian-type) dolls in her 1964 book, *A New Guide for Collectors.* She states: "The history of the bisque doll head parallels the history of the chinas. However, there is more variety in the kind of bisque than in the kind of china used for doll parts. One such variety, the so-called 'Parian' for dolls, is nothing more than highly polished, basically un-colored bisque, but the name makes a convenient handle for collectors to use. A careful study of Parian bisque pieces in accredited museums throughout the country will show the difference between what collectors call Parian as applied to dolls, and genuine Parian."

In the 1995 *UFDC List of Accepted Terms,* we find these dolls defined as follows: "Parian doll: doll made of fine white bisque (unglazed porcelain) without tinting. The features, hair and cheeks may be painted. Occasionally, these dolls have glass eyes." *The Random House Dictionary of the English Language* defines the word tint as "a delicate or pale color." As doll collectors, we refer to a doll head as a "tinted head" whether it has an overall complexion coat of light pink or darker flesh color. (After tinting, the facial features such as eyebrows, eyes and mouths were painted.)

The first group of dolls I have listed as "parians" are

Introduction

2. This 13½-inch parian-like figurine represents a Greek goddess. Gods and goddesses were popular subjects for the original life-size marble statues made of Paros marble. Author's Collection. (Photo: Gregg Smith)

3. The two 9½-inch parian-like busts, right and left in this photograph, resemble the types of busts shown at The London International Exhibition of 1851. The stark-white un-tinted bisque surface of the busts makes an ideal background for the pastel head painting. The 5½-inch parian-like shoulder head, center, was made from a master mold identical to the head/shoulders of the doll on the left in the photograph. Author's Collection. (Photo: Gregg Smith)

4. The A.W. Fr. Kister porcelain factory made this pair of 13½-inch parian-like figurines with painted heads. The head painting resembles that found on the majority of un-tinted bisque shoulder heads. Note the typical Kister painted mouth. The upper lip is narrow with low wide-spaced peaks and the lower lip is identical to many found on Kister parian-like dolls. Author's Collection. (Photo: Gregg Smith)

un-tinted bisque dolls. They are easily recognized because the faces and shoulder plates are stark white, without color of any kind except for the painted features. In other words, they are not "tinted" dolls because the complexion coat is absent.

The second group of dolls we must consider including under the definition "parians" are dolls with a very pale-pink complexion coat on their faces and/or shoulder plates. The majority of these dolls are similar in modeling and facial painting to the un-tinted bisque dolls made in the 1860s and 1870s, except for the overall application of a pale color over the entire face and shoulder plate. For the purposes of this book, I refer to these dolls as "parian-like."

The third group of dolls I've included in this book, for the sake of comparison, are bisque dolls. On these dolls, factory workers applied an overall flesh-colored complexion coat under the facial painting.

In the early 1840s, several English potteries experimented with kiln-firing a porcelain mixture that resulted in fine-textured, white porcelain, which resembled the marble from Paros. William Taylor Copeland and Thomas Battam, art director for the Copeland porcelain factory, are credited with creating the first parian ware. During the same time period, the Minton and Wedgwood porcelain factories made similar white un-tinted bisque.

In 1847 the Copeland porcelain factory advertised: "Parian Ware, statuary porcelain which is meant to look like the marble taken from Paros, the island where Greek and Roman marble was mined." English parian ware was

INTRODUCTION

4

Introduction

5. An original fashion illustration from *Godey's Lady's Book* shows some of the hairstyles worn during the 1860s. The caption reads: "Godey's Fashions for September 1867." Thuringian porcelain factories often looked to hairstyles worn by models in fashion illustrations as inspiration for molded-hair dolls. Author's Collection.

first introduced to the world at The London International Exhibition of 1851, where manufactured goods from all over the world were on display. The parian-ware statuary at the exhibition included 14-15-inch copies of the life-sized ancient Paros marble statues. English artists and sculptors used literary heroines, Bible stories, paintings and many other sources as subjects for their parian ware. The small statues and busts were among the most admired decorative objects on display at the exhibition. This is especially noteworthy because manufacturers from all over the world displayed their finest wares at this first International Exhibition.

It is helpful to know a little about the Victorian era to understand why there was such a market for parian ware. The Victorian era dates from the 1834 birth of the English Queen Victoria to her death in 1901. England was an extremely prosperous country during the sixty-seven-year reign of Victoria. Worldwide markets were developing, due to improved transportation and communication. British factories began to produce a wide variety of products to sell to customers in these new markets. The London International Exhibition of 1851 was a perfect venue for exhibiting the newest British products in a magnificent setting.

Representatives of many Thuringian porcelain factories attended the London event. They were immediately aware of the attention the small parian-ware statues and busts were receiving. While glazed-porcelain doll heads had been on the market since they were introduced by KPM Meissen in 1836, this exciting new product was especially appealing to porcelain-factory owners because it was inexpensive to produce. It was also an ideal medium for creating fine sculptured details.

The white un-tinted shoulder heads were the perfect background for maximum creative expression. The matte finish showcased the detailed modeling of the heads and

Introduction

6. This 1871 original fashion illustration from *Peterson's Magazine* shows the change in hairstyles from the previous decade. The main difference was the exaggerated hairstyle height above the crown, which became popular in the 1870s. The caption reads: "Les Modes Parisiennes Peterson's Magazine December 1871." Author's Collection.

shoulder plates. Many 1860s and 1870s parian-like dolls resemble elegant ladies. The elaborate hairstyles include molded ringlets, braids, molded combs, head bands, beads and Dresden-like flowers. The shoulder plates often feature molded jewelry and blouse details like ruffles, ribbons and bows.

The late toy curator John Noble aptly describes the elaborately decorated hairstyles and shoulder plates on parian-like "fancies" in his 1967 book titled *Dolls*. Noble writes: "The dolls seem to have come to the full bloom of their popularity in the early 1870's, a time of luscious and flowery fashions. The different hairstyles and decorations to be found on the heads are seemingly endless—festoons of curls, loops and braids and bangs, combs and jewels, flowers, ribbons and wreaths, all arranged with taste and exuberance. Many have yokes or collars of frilled embroidery molded on their shoulders, as well as modeled necklaces, while real earrings hang from their pierced ears.

"The coloring is pastel and sugary, the skin left dazzling white, with pale blond hair, while the features and trimmings are delicately tinted. On some examples, ribbons and other trimmings have been glazed, with very rich effect. Occasionally there is black or dark brown hair, making a startling contrast, but the pale icing-sugar look was far more successful. There is a variety which has a pink-flesh tint—these have been called 'French Parians,' a pretty name, but implying a provenance by no means certain. Heads were sold alone, especially for exporting, but complete dolls were also made, and these have matching limbs, the feet shod with the most elegant gilt tasseled boots.

"It is difficult to remember that these enchanting dolls were made in quantity and sold comparatively cheaply. Some heads with their original sales stickers intact have shown prices between twenty-five and fifty cents. In the 1870s these were considerable sums to spend on a child's

Introduction

7. Five Kestner dollhouse dolls illustrate the difference in parian-like and bisque shoulder heads. The lady doll in the center has a very pale complexion coat and, in my opinion, is a parian-like doll. The male doll on the far right has slightly more tinting, yet I consider him a parian-like doll. The three other dolls have bisque shoulder heads. For comparison, look at the stark-white untinted bisque lower legs on the two lady dolls. Also see illustrations 13, 14 and 16 in the Kestner chapter for an even better comparison. Author's collection. (Photo: Kirtley Krombholz)

toy, and such a doll, made up and carefully dressed by Mama, might well be a little girl's 'best' doll, to be cherished and played with. But this is a far cry from the costly Dresden and Nymphenburg figurines with which they have often been classed. Nevertheless, the Parians achieved a peak of excellence in doll making which has perhaps never been matched."

Little accurate dating information has surfaced regarding early unmarked bisque shoulder-head dolls made in Thuringia. The exact date a particular shoulder-head mold was introduced or retired is unknown. Work-related details concerning Thuringian porcelain factories are also almost nonexistent. It is very rare to find written records describing daily life inside a porcelain factory. Fortunately, in 1996 a group of Sonneberg area workers gave oral histories relating to doll and porcelain work during the boom years of dollmaking. A 1996 book by Angelika Tessmer that contains these important recollections is titled *Sonneberger Geschichten, Von Puppen, Griffeln, und Kuckuckspfeifen, Aus der Arbeitswelt unserer Grosseltern* (Sonneberg Stories of Dolls, Slate Pencils and Cuckoo Whistles, From the Workaday World of our Grandparents). Oral accounts from Tessmer's book are featured in this book. Thousands of Thuringian workers were responsible for making the antique dolls we collect today. By "walking a mile" in their shoes through descriptive word pictures, we gain a better understanding of the joys and hardships of making porcelain dolls in Thuringia.

Although it has been many years since porcelain-head dolls were made, specific information continues to surface regarding the manufacturing of these dolls. I am very fortunate to have uncovered more than one thousand shards that show the distinctive facial painting used by each Thuringian factory described in this book. By comparing undamaged shoulder-heads with identical facial painting to my shards, I am able to identify the majority of parian-like dolls for the first time. The molded hairstyles on the dolls allow me to date the dolls by decade, while my extensive collection of original porcelain factory ledgers and sample books confirms the makers of these beautiful dolls.

Chapter 1

Porcelain Dollmaking in Germany

1. This photograph shows the villages of Scheibe, Alsbach, Limbach and Steinheid. The A.W. Fr. Kister porcelain factory was located in the neighboring villages of Scheibe and Alsbach. The quarry in Steinheid supplied much of the kaolin (porcelain clay) used in the Thuringian porcelain factories. (Photo: Mary Krombholz)

Porcelain is made up of approximately one-half white china clay (kaolin) that does not discolor under high temperatures, one-fourth quartz (a mineral that is the chief constituent of sand and other rocks) and one-fourth feldspar. Feldspar is also a mineral found in certain rocks formed under conditions of intense heat. Kaolin is granite that turns to clay after a long period of decomposition. There are many grades of kaolin, and they vary in price according to the purity and whiteness that occurs after kiln firing.

One recipe for Thuringian hard-paste porcelain is forty to sixty percent kaolin, twenty to thirty percent quartz and twenty to thirty percent feldspar. Recipes varied between porcelain factories. Two quarries in the Kamm region of Thuringia contain kaolin that results in extremely white porcelain products. The two quarries, located in the small villages of Steinheid and Neuhaus, provided the majority of kaolin necessary to create doll-related porcelain products in Thuringian porcelain factories. Kaolin, quartz and feldspar were ground in a mill to a specific degree of fineness in order for the three elements to fuse together during firing. The particles had to be the same size, or they would not mix evenly. The finer the parts of a porcelain mixture were ground, the finer the quality of the resulting bisque. Years ago, water-powered grinding wheels were used to grind the porcelain mixture.

Kaolin is the only one of the porcelain elements that is pliable. The more pliable the mixture became, the

Chapter 1

2. The porcelain factory in Stützhaus was used at different times by the Alt, Beck & Gottschalck and Hertel, Schwab porcelain factories. The storage building in the foreground is constructed of discarded plaster molds supported by wooden beams. Plaster molds were desirable because they were an inexpensive waterproof substitute for costly building materials. (Photo: Christiane Gräfnitz)

3. This old wooden potter's wheel brings to mind the porcelain factory modelers who used a foot pedal to create original doll-head models of clay on the turning surface. (Photo: Mary Krombholz)

more successfully it retained the shape of the mold. During the 1860s and 1870s, factory workers spent a great deal of time kneading the clay mixture. Later on, machines replaced hand labor. Regardless of the way the clay mixture was kneaded, it was very pliable at this point, and did not lose this property when water was added to the clay-like mixture to make porcelain slip. The completed casting slip (*Giesschlicker*) was poured into plaster working molds. The porcelain mixture was considered clay until it was fired. It then became unglazed porcelain (bisque).

When exposed to the heat of a kiln, feldspar not only melts and fills the pores of the kaolin, it also fuses with the quartz. Quartz is harder than steel. Porcelain is durable because of the fusing of its component parts. The main difference between soft- and hard-paste porcelain is the difference in kiln temperature required to produce each type of porcelain. Hard-paste porcelain is fired at a minimum of 2,515 degrees Fahrenheit.

Porcelain Dollmaking

4. In the 1990s it was common to find thousands of plaster working molds stored in Thuringian porcelain factory attics. In 1995 the Weiss, Kühnert & Co. porcelain factory in Gräfenthal had thirty thousand molds stored in four separate attics. It was a thrill to study many half-doll molds when I spent two days and nights at the factory in 1998. German Doll Company partners Susan Bickert and Roland Schlegel rented the factory for many years. (Photo: Mary Krombholz)

Designing the Doll Head

Porcelain dolls have always been purchased or rejected by buyers depending on the appeal of each doll head. Talented artists whose designs sold well were in demand at every Thuringian porcelain factory. Artists employed by a porcelain factory either worked full time at the factory or were hired on a freelance basis. Artists often worked for more than one porcelain factory. It is understandable that shoulder heads from different porcelain factories may bear a slight resemblance to each other, because the same artist may have designed them.

The first step in the production of a porcelain doll head was to commission an artist/designer to create an original drawing. Artists often used sculptures or paintings from earlier centuries as inspiration for doll-head designs. Artists were also inspired to design a doll head by studying the head shape and facial contours of a family member or friend. If the drawing was approved by the factory owner(s), it was turned over to a sculptor (referred to as a modeler) who made a three-dimen-

5. During the 1860s and 1870s, porcelain shoulder heads were fired in large round beehive kilns. Very few old kilns exist in Thuringia today. (Photo: Christiane Gräfnitz)

Chapter 1

6. This is a master mold for a A.W. Fr. Kister shoulder head with a modified Flat Top hairstyle. The surface of the plaster mold is coated with shellac to aid in removal of the working molds. (Photo: Mary Krombholz)

7. This is the plaster working mold made from the master mold seen in illustration 6. (Photo: Mary Krombholz)

sional model of the drawing, using clay and a potter's wheel. Original models could also be made of plaster and, occasionally, wood.

Modeling

In her book *Modern Porcelain, Today's Treasures, Tomorrow's Traditions*, author Alberta Trimble describes the role of a modeler in the following way: "Modelers used their artistic talents and hand dexterity to transform a damp lump of clay into a humanlike image. The original mold, either in clay or plaster of Paris, is made from the drawing of a designer, an important person who thoroughly understands all the processes, for example how the different clays react and which temperature serves the clay best. He works in collaboration with the various departments to ensure that what began as a gleam in his eye becomes a visible object in the marketplace."

Modelers were required to allow for the amount of shrinkage that occurred as the wet clay of the original shoulder head model dried. Shrinkage also took place after the porcelain mixture was poured or pressed into a plaster working mold. A last shrinkage occurred during the firing of a doll head. The finest porcelain shoulder heads were created by experienced modelers who were aware of the problems in design caused by shrinkage. A sculpted mouth or nose could change considerably due to the amount of shrinkage. There is no question that antique dolls are more valuable today if the facial details were initially well defined and the molds used to make the heads were not worn.

Mold Making

By studying the plaster molds used to create shoulder heads, we gain an understanding of the difficulties encountered by mold makers and pourers. A master mold (often referred to as a 'mother' mold in Germany) is made from each side of an original clay model. A master mold is a mirror image of the original model because the image of the doll heads and parts are raised above the flat sides of the mold. Each half of the mold is coated with shellac to preserve the plaster surface of the mold. Master molds are used over and over again to make plaster working molds.

Working molds are negative molds. In other words, the mold image is recessed. Each time porcelain slip is poured into a working mold, the surface of the mold wears. This results in a less-defined doll head, with the loss of many finer molding details. KPM Meissen porcelain-factory workers currently use a working mold thirty to forty times before discarding the mold.

Pouring (Casting) and Turning

The two or more parts of a plaster working mold were held together with elastic bands or string to keep the pieces from separating as the mold pourer filled the mold. Pourers (also called casters) poured the slip into the opening of the plaster of Paris mold. The creamy consistency of the porcelain slip allowed it to be poured into the molds. As the water in the slip was absorbed by the porous plaster surface of the mold, a thin layer of the clay mixture was deposited on the interior surfaces of the mold. It was necessary to add more casting slip to the mold as the mixture settled and began to adhere to the interior surfaces of the mold. After a short length of time, the mold was inverted to allow the surplus slip to drain out. At many Thuringian porcelain factories in earlier centuries, the surplus slip was poured into a hole in a second-floor molding-room floor to a container resting on the floor below. By adding water to thin the thickened slip, the slip could be recycled.

As a thin layer of clay adhered to the walls of the mold, it formed a membrane. The clay changed from a wet, shiny substance to a slightly dull substance. After a short time, an average of about one-quarter inch of deposited clay was visible around the opening of the mold. An experienced worker knew when to remove the slightly hardened clay membrane from the mold. To determine when to remove the object from the mold, the worker touched the surface surrounding the mold opening to see if his finger left a fingerprint. When a fingerprint was no longer visible on the semi-soft clay, it was time to un-mold the object.

During the years that parian-like dolls were made, a turner cut the surplus clay from the opening of the mold and carefully removed the shoulder head inside. At this point in the production process, the shoulder head resembled leather. The surplus clay surrounding the mold seams was taken off with a knife. Eye cuts were also made at this time, if the doll order called for glass eyes.

8. This group of discarded plaster working molds was made from the master mold shown in illustration 6. (Photo: Mary Krombholz)

9. This work table in an upstairs room was where workers in the old Alt, Beck & Gottschalck factory in Stützhaus poured slip into the opening of the plaster molds, un-molded the slightly hardened clay membrances and cut surplus clay from the mold seams. (Photo: Christiane Gräfnitz)

Chapter 1

10. This fine example of a parian shoulder head with a fancy hairstyle was recently found at the old Alt, Beck & Gottschalck porcelain factory building in Stützhaus by Wolfgang Ortlepp, current owner of the property. Mary Krombholz Collection. (Photo: Christiane Gräfnitz)

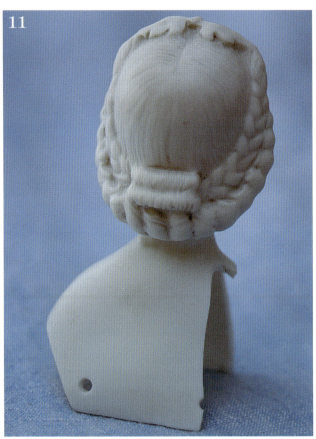

11. The back view of the un-tinted bisque shard points out the fine quality of the porcelain that showcases each detail of the elaborate hairstyle. Mary Krombholz Collection. (Photo: Christiane Gräfnitz)

Assembling, Fettling, Firing and Sanding

When the shoulder head was dry enough to be handled without causing damage, an assembler attached the separate parts of the mold, using porcelain slip as glue. Ornamentation, such as molded jewelry, porcelain ruffles, ribbons and flowers, was applied by hand, using porcelain slip as an adhesive. The word "fettled" was used to describe the cleaning of a dry shoulder head before it was kiln fired. A shoulder head was fettled with a metal tool or a special sponge to remove the surface imperfections. Following the bisque firing, the unglazed porcelain object was sanded. The sanding step was extremely important because it smoothed the slightly rough surface of the fired porcelain. At each stage of production, the shoulder head was inspected to determine if it was warped, contained iron specks or had other blemishes.

It is difficult to imagine how complicated the process of firing porcelain was during the years these doll heads were made. The same amount of wood or coal had to be added to each of the kiln fireplaces in order to create even heat in the kiln. Although doll heads felt dry to the touch, moisture inside a head caused one of the greatest problems that could occur during bisque firing. Doll heads often contained small air bubbles, which were left following the kneading process. This was disastrous because the bubbles exploded during firing. Many of the doll-head shards in my collection reflect the damage caused by pockets of air in the pouring slip.

It was also important that the kiln temperature increase slowly during the first part of the firing so that the last vestiges of water in the porcelain could be released without damaging the object. The entire contents of a beehive kiln could be destroyed by a small error in kiln temperature.

A Steinbach porcelain-factory worker provides important information on beehive-kiln firing in his oral history, contained in Angelika Tessmer's *Sonneberger Geschi-*

12. In the late nineteenth century, "turners" un-molded porcelain from working molds, trimmed the excess porcelain from the mold seams, and cut out eye and mouth openings. This 1880 photograph shows fourteen Kestner & Co. turners. Photo: Courtesy Ohrdruf Town Museum.

chten, Von Puppen, Griffeln, und Kuckuckspfeifen, Aus der Arbeitswelt unserer Grosseltern (Sonneberg Stories of Dolls, Slate Pencils and Cuckoo Whistles, From the Workaday World of our Grandparents). He explains: "The heart of the factory was the firing department. The oven was dome shaped. Around the oven were six fireplaces in even distances. The hot gases were channeled through canals in the oven wall to the highest point in the dome where those canals met and formed a chimney. The porcelain was stored in firing capsules made of *Schamotte* (a fireproof ceramic container). The filled capsules were closed up and arranged in a circle in the firing chamber.

"The rougher electrical or sanitary (bathroom) porcelain was placed in the outer circle, close to the fireplaces, which had the highest temperatures. The fine decorative porcelain was placed on the inside. When the oven was full, a *Schamotte* brick wall was put up to cover the oven door and seal the leaks off. One mistake in the placement of the porcelain in the kiln resulted in the loss of valuable merchandise. Experienced workers were always in charge of the firing process."

The Steinbach porcelain-factory worker also sheds light on the process of firing doll heads by the majority of Thuringian porcelain factories. "Somehow the firer had to determine when the temperature was high enough and when the firing had been long enough. There were no set times, and the quality and the heating power of coal varied and played a significant role during firing. Their trick was to place a sample piece and three

Chapter 1

13. These stacked firing capsules (*Schamotte*) remind us of the many years doll-related porcelain was enclosed inside fireproof ceramic containers to protect it from the uneven heat and dust inside the kiln during firing. (Photo: Mary Krombholz)

'*Segerkegel*' on top of a capsule by the window. One brick was left loose at eye level to serve as a window into the kiln.

"The *Segerkegel* looked like thin porcelain sticks. They were partially inserted into a blob of porcelain *Masse* on top of a capsule by the window. When the temperature reached 800 degrees Centigrade, the first *Kegel* broke. At 1000 degrees centigrade, the second *Kegel* broke. At 1400 degrees Centigrade, the last *Kegel* broke and the correct firing temperature had been reached." *Segerkegel* (kiln-sitters) were invented by ceramist Hermann Seger. They are 5-6 centimeter-high slim pyramid-shaped cones that are used to indicate different melting points from 600 to 2000 degrees Centigrade. They bend over when proper heat is reached. The Meissen porcelain factory continues to use *Segerkegel* during the second firing, which requires the highest kiln temperature. The firing of 1860s and 1870s parian-like shoulder heads was especially difficult because *Segerkegel* were not invented until 1886.

"The length of the firing was determined by the sample piece. The firer would get it through the window in the kiln wall, and test it by knocking it. The sound told him whether the firing process was finished or if it had to be fired longer. One had to be very careful during the firing. Once all six fireplaces were burning, one put on three or four shovels full of coal in each fireplace. The oven temperature was not allowed to rise too quickly, or the goods would crack.

"Slowly, the firing increased to 5-7 shovels full. After the warming up phase was completed, the temperature of 1400 degrees Centigrade was reached. Then the '*Sharfbrennen*' (sharp firing) could begin. It lasted 12 to 14 hours. The risk of cooling too quickly and cracking the goods was also great. Slowly the firers started taking down a few bricks out of the wall. The temperature was so great that flames would shoot out of the firing chamber. The *Schamotte* firing capsules were emptied and the goods were checked for cracks and sorted, before they were sent to the painting department. Following the painting steps, the pieces of porcelain were fired again at a lower temperature to make the colors permanent. The porcelain products were then taken to an inventory room, where the objects were inspected for flaws before they were shipped to buyers."

Alberta Trimble, author of *Modern Porcelain, Today's Treasures, Tomorrow's Traditions,* visited many English porcelain factories in search of information for her book. She writes: "The fire is the magician that transfigures all this lifeless material. It is the fundamental factor in the whole process of manufacture and is, therefore, also the one that strikes the spectator most. In the ceramic industry there is an added tension during the actual firing, which creates a special atmosphere fraught with excitement.

"In the oven, the ultimate reward will be determined and the question is, will all the preceding efforts be rewarded, or will the work be irrevocably wasted? When the ware is being 'placed' in or 'drawn' from the kiln, there is always a tremendous bustle. In some mysterious way the rumor of what is going on spreads all over the factory; you will see artists and technicians, the kiln men and the young apprentices rushing up to ask the news, to peer in the kiln, and to return satisfied to their various posts if everything seemed to be progressing favorably. It is their sum of common interests that is at stake."

A Year in the Life of a German Doll Manufacturer

It was difficult for a Thuringian porcelain factory located in a small, secluded town to understand the changing world markets and to continually introduce new doll-head styles year after year. The most important venue for

14. Once the porcelain was enclosed in firing capsules and placed inside the kiln, it was important to carefully monitor the kiln temperatures to ensure they reached the levels that would produce hard-paste porcelain. Two small cone-shaped *Segerkegels*, placed on top of the plaster mold at the far right on the shelf in this photograph, were used to gauge kiln temperatures. (Photo: Mary Krombholz)

the introduction of new styles was the semi-annual Leipzig Fair. Attendance at the Leipzig Fairs was a "must" for manufacturers and buyers who were interested in promoting and selling doll-related porcelain products. We have some documentation on doll exports in the early 1800s, which tells us that in those years doll exports from Sonneberg totaled 300,000 to 500,000 a year. From the 1880s until World War I, several million dolls were exported yearly from the Sonneberg area alone. During the 1860s and 1870s, porcelain-head dolls led the list of exports in Katzhütte, Gräfenhain, Nauendorf, Ohrdruf and Scheibe-Alsbach.

F.W. Woolworth, founder of the large chain of American "Five and Dime" stores, wrote a diary of a trip he made to Germany in 1890. His April 14th entry is as follows: "Get out of the way, hustle up, tumble up, confusion. That is Leipzig during the Fair. Leipzig is a city of 150,000 inhabitants, but now there are also 100,000 strangers. They call it a Fair but it is not like our Fairs. Thousands of manufacturers from all over the world rent rooms as near to the heart of the city as possible, at very high prices, and bring samples of their goods for sale." On April 17th, Woolworth made the following entry in his diary: "If anyone likes hard work and lots of it, let them come here and look over samples all day, up and down stairs, jostled about in crowded halls and sample rooms."

That was the point of view of the American buyer. For the doll manufacturers, the Leipzig Fair was just one part of their busy year. It is fortunate for doll collectors that Hanns Schoenau wrote an article for a 1997 issue of the *Ciesliks' Puppenmagazin*, detailing a year in the life of a doll manufacturer. Hanns Schoenau inherited the Schoenau & Hoffmeister porcelain factory near Sonneberg from his father, who had inherited it from his father. Schoenau studied his father's and grandfather's business records in order to explain the yearly activities relating to doll production from 1900 until about 1930.

From Hanns Schoenau's detailed account, I have chosen the sections that are of most interest to antique doll collectors to explain doll manufacturing from an owner's point of view. Schoenau wrote: "We begin with January. On the 1st of January, Sonneberg doll manufacturers

15. This old photograph shows two porcelain factory workers, wearing long white work aprons, stacking firing capsules inside a beehive kiln. (Photo: Courtesy Reichmannsdorf Porcelain Factory)

Chapter 1

16. A glazed-porcelain shoulder head, recently found by Wolfgang Ortlepp at the Alt, Beck & Gottschalck porcelain factory in Stützhaus, is posed with an identical, but larger, plaster working mold. Finds like this are becoming rarer and rarer because most of the Thuringian porcelain factories that made doll-related porcelain have been torn down. The Alt, Beck & Gottschalck factory building in Stützhaus is scheduled for demolition in the near future. Christiane Gräfnitz Collection. (Photo: Christiane Gräfnitz)

17. To complete this uncommon Alt, Beck & Gottschalck shoulder head, workers made precise eye and head cuts while the porcelain was in the leather stage. The measurements for the metal headband had to be extremely accurate so the two end pieces would fit into the holes between the hair puffs. Margaret Hartshorn Collection. (Photo: Image Arts Etc.)

traveled to London, Manchester, Liverpool, Birmingham and Glasgow, Scotland, to sales shows held mostly in hotels. In February, the manufacturers begin planning for the Leipzig Trade Show. The manufacturers also travel to Switzerland, Holland and Belgium. With many orders for dolls secured, the manufacturers give out material to home workers, including heads made of porcelain, fabric, stamped cardboard (for boxes), hair, voice boxes, celluloid accessories and other material.

"In March, the doll manufacturers travel to the Leipzig Trade Show. Also, the models for next year's production are planned with the help of artists and modelers. In April, after Easter, production is running 'full speed.' Warehouse space is ordered, doll orders are placed, and much more help is hired if business is good. In May, additional orders are solicited. There may be another trip to England and France. Visits are made to big German customers. And, wholesale and foreign representatives visit Sonneberg for business talks.

"June, July and August are vacation months. The manufacturer goes hunting or on a vacation with his family. Production must run smoothly. Packaged orders are transported and stored near the train station. In September, the doll manufacturers attend the Leipzig Fall Show. It is not as busy as the Spring Show. Production and delivery are in high gear. Home workers are putting in much overtime, especially the eye setters, the hairdressers and the voice makers. Market research is done. Trends are being studied in order to decide on next year's collection of dolls. Big wooden crates are delivered daily. In October, delivery runs in high

18. The Ohrdruf Town Museum is a treasure trove of photographs and records from the factories that made porcelain in the Ohrdruf area. This photograph shows a group of Alt, Beck & Gottschalck "painting ladies" with their teacher. Courtesy Ohrdruf Town Museum.

gear. The first samples are finished for the year ahead. Samples and collections are shipped to the main customers overseas.

"In November, the planning for the collection introduced the following year is completed. The manufacturers and sales representatives travel to Europe again, especially England, France, Brussels, Amsterdam, and Switzerland. The latest doll models are introduced at the big department stores like Woolworth, Kresge, Butler Brothers and Borgfeldt. The sample room is decorated. Production is still running in high gear. Back orders of catalog and specialty sales are filled. Everybody is in a rush. No one has any time. Every person works 15 to 18 hours a day. The children help. Freight is coming from Neustadt or Mengersgereuth. The train station is very busy. Delivery people are standing in line at drop-off counters. At the end of the month, life begins to quiet down a little. Manufacturers take some time to go hunting or celebrate an anniversary at the local *Wirthaus* (pub).

"In December, the factories are quiet. Doll inventories are taken, invoices are written and plans for vacations are announced. The doll collection going to England is packed up, so that the manufacturers can travel there right after the holidays are over. Sales representatives visit the doll factories to show fabrics, mohair, lace, ribbon, stamped cardboard, cardboard boxes, plush (to make stuffed animals), celluloid, stencils, and other supplies.

"The rich traders and manufacturers concentrate on the anniversary of the *'Erholungs Gesellschaft'* (club of manufacturers established in the twenties of the 19th Century) on the 17th of December. Hairdressers and tailors go from house to house, and the day of celebration is enjoyed thoroughly. On the holidays, the children of the poorer families go around and ask for leftover toys. On Christmas Eve, it was the custom at the doll factory Arthur Schoenau to put a big crate outside the factory gate filled with dolls. Every person is allowed to take what he or she wants."

The Porcelain Factories

25

Chapter 2
Alt, Beck & Gottschalck

1. This 1854 brick building in Nauendorf housed the first Alt, Beck & Gottschalck porcelain factory. According to the book *The Thuringian Industry* in 1888, the first Thuringian bisque shoulder heads were made in a kiln on the ground floor of this building. A painter's studio was located on the second floor. The historic old building is still standing today on the original factory site. (Photo: Mary Krombholz)

Alt, Beck & Gottschalck porcelain shoulder heads were made at two factory buildings in Nauendorf and one factory building in Stützhaus. The first factory building was built in 1854. It is described in an article titled "White Gold from Nauendorf," written by Jürgen and Marianne Cieslik, which was published in the doll magazine *Puppenmagazin* in the August 26, 2001, issue. The Ciesliks tell of the founding of the factory: "Once upon a time, there were four poor porcelain workers. They worked in the Kling porcelain factory in Ohrdruf and together they dreamed of fortune and success. They were young, enthusiastic and passionate in their profession." The four men received permission to produce porcelain on March 6, 1854. Carl Ehrenberger, Theodor Gottschalck and Heinrich Volker were former Kling porcelain turners and Gottlieb Beck was a modeler. In 1854 they built a small brick factory on Ehrenberger's property and hired what must have been a good number of workers, considering there were sixty-eight documented workers two years later, in 1856. During the first few months they had many problems and arguments relating to porcelain firing in the small round kiln. According to the Ciesliks: "The first firings were a disaster and no one knew why. The first factory employees had to be let go. There was a quarrel among the owners. Carl Ehrenberger was the first to leave the group. He sold his shares to Gottschalck and Beck. They also had to use the money to pay Voelker's debt, who had failed to inform the partners of the company's bad financial situation. After six months, only Beck and Gottschalck remained of the original owners."

Gottlieb Beck and Theodor Gottschalck were not dis-

2. The second Alt, Beck and Gottschalck porcelain factory building is located on the same factory site in Nauendorf as the building pictured in illustration 1. This building has been remodeled to provide housing for village residents. (Photo: Mary Krombholz)

couraged. They worked hard to develop a recipe for bisque dolls heads, and were successful in finding customers for their new product. In their 2001 article, the Ciesliks also shed light on Alt's role in the factory. "Impressed by the success of these two young factory owners, brick factory owner and later commerce counselor Johann George Wilhelm Alt bought into the company. He was 75 years old. With his financial help, the company could expand."

Some problems were difficult to solve. Beck and Gottschalck could not afford a *Masse* mill to grind the porcelain elements of kaolin, quartz and feldspar. (The word *Masse* refers to the porcelain mixture; these mills were initially powered by water from the fast-moving mountain streams found on the grounds of porcelain factories.) Therefore, they had to use a porcelain slab and a grinding stone to hand-grind each individual component of the porcelain mixture. Hand grinding was difficult work, but it resulted in extremely fine textured, smooth porcelain. During the first year of production, Beck and Gottschalck worked out a proportion of elements and firing techniques to create unglazed porcelain (bisque).

The discovery of Thuringia's first bisque recipe is described in a book titled *The Thuringian Industry* in 1888: "With the introduction of this progressive innovation, the little company turned out to be successful. Porcelain children were first introduced to the market by this Nauendorf factory." In regard to this 1888 book, the Ciesliks state: "These historic sources do not prove, but they suggest that according to known quotes from this book, Beck and Gottschalck were the inventors of biscuit porcelain." In my opinion, among the first un-tinted bisque heads produced by this factory were the Empress Eugenie shoulder heads shown in illustrations 6 and 7 on page 30. The bisque on these heads is so much smoother than that on heads made after ABG began using a *Masse* mill that it seems clear the *Masse* must have been ground by hand. I can also date these dolls' heads to the early 1860s because so many have been found on the autoperipetikos walking bodies, which were patented in 1862.

In their 2001 article, the Ciesliks list the Alt, Beck & Gottschalck porcelain workers' hometowns in 1856 as follows: "In 1856, it is recorded that the company employed 68 people; 29 from Ohrdruf, 21 from Gräfenhain, 15 from Nauendorf, 2 from Hohenkirchen and 1 from Georgenthal. This does not count the home work-

Chapter 2

3. This 1914 photograph shows the 104 male and female employees of the Hertel, Schwab & Co. porcelain factory. The two-story addition pictured in illustration 5 is evident behind the grouped employees. Courtesy Ohrdruf Museum.

ers." This list shows that many porcelain workers lived outside Nauendorf, but within walking or horse-pulled-wagon distance of the factory. The majority of residents of small villages and towns surrounding a Thuringian porcelain factory depended entirely on the factory for their quality of life.

Doll collectors are very familiar with the Nauendorf factory location, but few know that doll-related porcelain was also made in the Alt, Beck & Gottschalck factory located in Stützhaus (a suburb of Ohrdruf) from 1864 on. In their 2001 article, the Ciesliks provide information on the Alt, Beck & Gottschalck porcelain factories in Nauendorf and Stützhaus. "The new Nauendorf manager in 1869 was Christian E. Reinhold Weingart. Before taking over the Nauendorf factory, Weingart had been a co-owner of the Stützhaus porcelain factory, which was bought by Alt, Beck & Gottschalck in 1864. In 1881, Weingart became a co-owner of the Nauendorf factory. In 1911, it (the Alt, Beck & Gottschalck Stützhaus factory) was sold to Hertel, Schwab & Co."

Peter Cramer, curator of the Ohrdruf Town Museum, has researched the history of the Ohrdruf area porcelain factories for many years. His important research sheds new light on the Alt, Beck & Gottschalck and Hertel, Schwab & Co. porcelain factories. For example, among the holdings in the permanent collection of the Ohrdruf Town Museum archives is an Alt, Beck & Gottschalck letter dated 1895 with a letterhead listing the 52 Sulerstrasse address in Stützhaus as a second porcelain factory address. Another letter, the first in the Ohrdruf museum archives relating to the Hertel, Schwab & Co. porcelain factory is dated 1913 and the letterhead lists the 52 Sulerstrasse address in Stützhaus as the location of the Hertel, Schwab & Co. porcelain factory. From these doc-

4. The third Alt, Beck & Gottschalck porcelain factory building was located at 52 Sulerstrasse in Stützhaus, a suburb of Ohrdruf. The Alt, Beck, & Gottschalck porcelain factory made doll heads and parts in Stützhaus from 1864 on. (Photo: Christiane Gräfnitz)

5. In 1914 the Hertel, Schwab & Co. porcelain factory added a two-story addition to the old Alt, Beck & Gottschalck porcelain factory located at 52 Sulerstrasse in the Ohrdruf suburb of Stützhaus. Stützhaus is known as Luisenthal today because the villages of Stützhaus, Schwarzwald and Luisenthal merged a number of years ago. (Photo: Christiane Gräfnitz)

CHAPTER 2

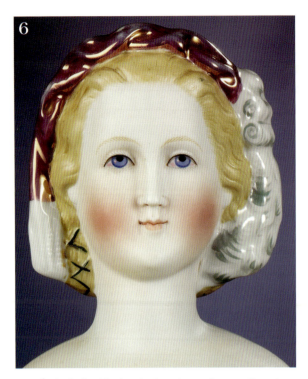

7. A close view of another 4½-inch shoulder head with an Empress Eugenie hairstyle and less cheek blushing shows the pale blond multi-stroke eyebrows, finely painted upper and lower eyelashes, light-blue painted eyes with glazed pupils and light-red lip painting with a darker-red lip accent line. As is typical with the majority of shoulder heads, the lip line dips into a small "V" in the center of the lips. The pageboy hairstyle has well-defined comb marks under the molded snood in back. Author's Collection. (Photo: Gregg Smith)

6. A 4½-inch shoulder head referred to as Empress Eugenie has a mauve luster scarf decorating her simple blond hairstyle. The entire headdress is glazed. A feather frames one side of the face, while a tassel adds interest to the other side of the face. A green molded snood covers the back hair. The eye painting includes blue painted eyes with glazed pupils, a thin black line outlining the upper eyelids, blond multi-stroke eyebrows and upper and lower eyelashes. The white spaces surrounding the irises are painted pink in this example. Olson/Nelson Collection. (Photo: Red Kite Studios)

8. This 5½-inch parian-like shoulder head with an Alice in Wonderland hairstyle has similar facial painting as the Empress Eugenies shown in illustrations 6 and 7. The slightly smiling mouth has a typical factory darker-red lip accent line. Fine brushstrokes are painted around the hairline. The blond hair is held in place by a mauve luster headband in front and a green molded snood in back. Estelle Johnston Collection. (Photo: Estelle Johnston)

9. In March 2004, Christiane Gräfnitz found these five porcelain shoulder head shards in the old Alt, Beck & Gottschalck porcelain factory in Stützhaus. They measure from 2 to 3½ inches in height.

30

10. This 2½-inch parian-like Empress Eugenie shoulder head is mounted on an original autoperipatetikos body. The walking mechanism was patented in 1862. The head has multi-stroke eyebrows, highlighted outlined blue irises and lower painted eyelashes. Susan Moore Collection. (Photo: Digital Images)

11. This Empress Eugenie dollhouse doll has a 1¾-inch shoulder head and a green molded snood covering the back of the well-defined hair. The pink luster scarf, feather and tassel are not glazed. Although the doll is identified as the Empress Eugenie, it does not resemble portraits of the wife of Napoleon III, who had long curly auburn hair. Ann Meehan Collection. (Photo: Curtis Haldy)

12. This 2-inch parian-like shoulder-head shard is pictured on the far left in illustration 9. It has a center-parted blond curly hairstyle and chubby cheeks. The head modeling and facial painting is typical of the shoulder heads made by the Alt, Beck & Gottschalck porcelain factories in Nauendorf and Stützhaus. Author's Collection (Photo: Gregg Smith)

13. At first glance, the twisted scarf, feathers and tassels molded on the blond hair seem to indicate this doll is an Empress Eugenie made by Alt, Beck and Gottschalck. But the well-defined upper eyelids that cover the top half circle of the pupils and the absence of a darker-red lip accent line suggest it was actually made by the Conta & Böhme porcelain factory. Estelle Johnston Collection. (Photo: Estelle Johnston)

14. These two unpainted shoulder heads were found under the floorboards of the Alt, Beck & Gottschalck porcelain factory in Nauendorf in the late 1980s. Hennelore Henze-Dollner Collection. (Photo: Christiane Gräfnitz)

15. The shoulder head on the left has long vertical curls while the one on the right has a snood-covered pageboy hairstyle. Hennelore Henze-Dollner Collection. (Photo: Christiane Gräfnitz)

16. This 3½-inch shoulder head made from a master mold identical to the one used for the example in illustration 17 has very fine textured un-tinted bisque. It differs from the Empress Eugenie shoulder head pictured in illustration 7 in several ways. This shoulder head with single-stroke eyebrows lacks the painted eyelashes, iris outlines or darker-red lip accent line of the Empress Eugenie. Author's Collection. (Photo: Red Kite Studios)

17. Long brown curls frame the face of this 3½-inch shoulder head with temple brushstrokes and a headband painted the same color as the hair. The parian-like shoulder head with vivid blue eyes was made from a master mold identical to the one used for unpainted shoulder head shown on the left in illustration 14. Terry Schmeltzer Collection. (Photo: Estelle Johnston)

Alt, Beck & Gottschalck

18. The pleated bodice on this 4½-inch shoulder head is trimmed with a ruffled collar and blue glazed ribbons at the neckline. The hairstyle has well-defined hair waves, long vertical curls and a black molded ribbon, which is barely visible in this photograph. Olson/Nelson Collection. (Photo: Red Kite Studios)

19. This 3½-inch shoulder head was made from a master mold identical to the example in illustration 18. The crossed-ribbon tie at the neckline is painted pink on this shoulder head. The back hairstyle contains a coiled roll of hair and long vertical curls. Terry Schmeltzer Collection. (Photo: Estelle Johnston)

20. A 2¾-inch 1870s Frozen Charlotte with blue boots was found at the Stützhaus porcelain factory in March 2004. The comb-marked blond hairstyle has a black headband modeled between the well-defined hair puffs. The body is slim compared to the A.W. Fr. Kister Frozen Charlottes pictured in illustrations 18 and 19 in chapter four. Author's Collection. (Photo: Gregg Smith)

21. This 3½-inch early shoulder head has the same type of smooth un-tinted bisque as the dolls shown in illustrations 6, 7, 8, and 16. Two large bows are attached to the headband. A molded snood covers the hair in back. The headband, bows and snood are painted the same color as the hair. Margaret Hartshorn Collection. (Photo: Image Arts Etc.)

33

22. This 4¾-inch parian-like shoulder-head doll has an original factory body and clothing. The head features include pierced ears with original earrings, blue glass eyes, upper and lower eyelashes and light-red lips with a darker-red lip accent line. Note the original un-tinted bisque lower legs with black-banded blue boots. Margaret Hartshorn Collection. (Photo: Image Arts Etc.)

23. Dolly Madison is the name given to shoulder heads with this ribbon-trimmed hairstyle. The molded headband and bow are painted the same color as the hair on this 5-inch parian-like shoulder head. Note the difference in hair color and headband width between this shoulder head and the Dolly Madison with the decorated shoulder plate in illustration 27. Olson/Nelson Collection. (Photo: Red Kite Studios)

24. The Alt, Beck & Gottschalck porcelain factory trimmed many fancy hairstyles with black or dark-blue molded ribbons. The hairstyle on this 4½-inch shoulder head contains a cluster of curls on the forehead and a black ribbon holding the long vertical curls in place in back. The head features include pierced ears, brown single-stroke eyebrows, glazed pupils and a V-shaped darker-red lip accent line. Olson/Nelson Collection. (Photo: Red Kite Studios)

25. This 3-inch shoulder head was made from a master mold identical to the one used for the doll in illustration 22. It has dark-blue glass eyes, a typical factory darker-red lip accent line, light-brown multi-stroke eyebrows, upper and lower painted eyelashes and pierced ears. The hairstyle includes an unusual arrangement of dark-blue ribbons that separate the smooth hair on the crown of the head from the molded curls in back. A strand of flat gold-painted beads encircles the neck. Terry Schmeltzer Collection. (Photo: Estelle Johnston)

26. This dollhouse doll with a 2½-inch shoulder head was made from a master mold identical to that used for the shoulder head in illustration 24. The pierced ears and separate headbands are the same on both dolls. Side-glancing eyes give the dollhouse doll a slightly different appearance. Ann Meehan Collection. (Photo: Curtis Haldy)

27 A master mold similar to the one used for the shoulder head in illustration 23 was used to make this uncommon Dolly Madison with a gold-trimmed rose luster hair ribbon and bow. The 4¼-inch shoulder head has applied details on the shoulder plate. Unlike the C.F. Kling porcelain factory, the Alt, Beck & Gottschalck porcelain factory seldom decorated shoulder plates on parian-like dolls. The neck ruffle adds to the decorative effect of the hand painted scrolls on each side of the gold-trimmed bodice opening. The applied ruffle is also hand painted. Olson/Nelson Collection. (Photo: Red Kite Studios)

uments, we can conclude that the 1860s and 1870s china and parian doll-head shards recently found at the Stützhaus porcelain factory were made by the Alt, Beck & Gottschalck porcelain factory rather than the Hertel, Schwab & Co. porcelain factory.

The Ohrdruf museum archival letters also substantiate the 1910 founding of the Hertel, Schwab & Co. porcelain factory. Although glazed porcelain doll heads have been attributed to this factory in doll books, we now have conclusive proof that the first porcelain-head dolls made by the Hertel, Schwab & Co. porcelain factory were flesh-tinted bisque character dolls.

In spring 2004 the well-known researcher Christiane Gräfnitz traveled to the village of Stützhaus (which today is known as Luisenthal, due to the merging of the villages) to photograph the old Alt, Beck & Gottschalck/ Hertel, Schwab & Co. porcelain factory for this book. The current owner of the old porcelain factory is Wolfgang Ortlepp, who bought the factory from the last Hertel, Schwab & Co. owner. He allowed Christiane to study a box of Alt, Beck & Gottschalck china and parian-like doll-head shards made in the 1860s and 1870s. They had been found under the floorboards in the oldest part of factory. He also gave Christiane a few of the shards to send to me for my research.

The shards are very important because they document doll-related porcelain that was previously unknown. Several of the doll-head shards are similar to well-known Alt, Beck & Gottschalck chinas. Others have glazed porcelain hairstyles that have not

18

This 6-inch Alice in Wonderland shoulder head was painted at a later time period than the Alice in illustration 8. This shoulder head is very well painted, but it lacks the extremely smooth bisque and fine eye, eyelash and mouth painting evident on the earliest dolls made by this factory. Olson/Nelson Collection. (Photo: Red Kite Studios)

Alt, Beck & Gottschalck

19. This 4½-inch shoulder head is marked with a large incised "8" on the back shoulder plate. The head features include a deep center part, short curly hair, single-stroke eyebrows, white iris highlights and a lip accent line that dips in the center to form the letter "V." Olson/Nelson Collection. (Photo: Red Kite Studios)

20. This 4¾-inch shoulder head has upswept blond hair and waves on each side of a center part. A dark-blue headband and exposed pierced ears are additional head features. Olson/Nelson Collection. (Photo: Red Kite Studios)

21. This lightly tinted parian-like doll with a 4-inch shoulder head has an asymmetrical hairstyle that is commonly found on glazed porcelain dolls. The large blue irises and small white iris highlights are identical on chinas and parians. The typical darker-red lip-accent line between the lips is visible in this photograph. Author's Collection. (Photo: Lee Krombholz)

22. This 5-inch shoulder head has pierced ears and loosely curled hair in front. The hairstyle is trimmed with a molded ribbon painted the same color as the hair. Another ribbon is woven through the curls in back. Olson/Nelson Collection. (Photo: Red Kite Studios)

CHAPTER 2

23. This 2½-inch shoulder head features a straw-like glazed pillbox hat trimmed with a triangular-shaped glazed white hat ornament trimmed in orange and gold. The facial features include blue painted eyes, single-stroke eyebrows and a darker-red lip accent line. The light- and dark-brown shaded hairstyle has thirteen vertical curls with a shorter curl on each side of the face in front. Margaret Hartshorn Collection. (Photo: Image Arts Etc.)

24. A back view of the shoulder head in illustration 23 shows how the hair shading accentuates the long vertical curls and comb-marked hairstyle. Margaret Hartshorn Collection. (Photo: Image Arts Etc.)

25. The Alt, Beck & Gottschalck porcelain factory created this 3-inch shoulder head with a similar glazed pillbox hat as the shoulder head in illustration 23. The childlike face and pale facial painting on the doll in illustration 23 are different from the short curly hair and more colorful facial painting on this example. Olson/Nelson Collection. (Photo: Red Kite Studios)

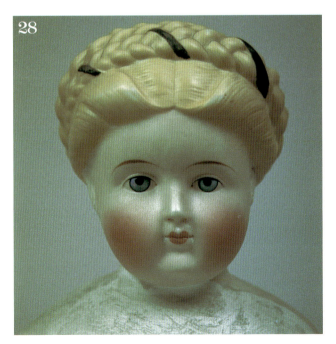

26. Uncommon hair shading is a focal point on this 3¾-inch glass-eyed shoulder head with an upswept hairdo and pierced ears. The facial painting includes multi-stroke eyebrows and dark-red lips with a darker-red lip accent line. A molded braid encircles the head while a thinner braid is tucked under the larger braid from ear to ear. A blue ribbon holds the braids in place. Margaret Hartshorn Collection. (Photo: Image Arts Etc.)

27. The back hairstyle of the shoulder head in illustration 26 includes a smoothly combed and shaded center section with a blue ribbon molded inside the circled braid. A molded bow hangs over the larger braid. Margaret Hartshorn Collection. (Photo: Image Arts Etc.)

28. This 5¾-inch shoulder head with blue painted eyes was made from a master mold similar to the one used for the doll in illustration 26. It is in the permanent collection of the Sonneberg Doll Museum. On this example, the facial painting is lighter in color and the blond hair is not shaded, which creates a different appearance. Courtesy Deutsches Spielzeugmuseum, Sonneberg. (Photo: Christiane Gräfnitz)

been attributed to this factory in the past. One glazed porcelain shoulder head with a fancy hairstyle may be one of the earliest chinas made by the factory. A head shard from a boy doll with a Kinderkopf hairstyle is also an example of early Alt, Beck & Gottschalck doll-related production.

I first noticed the unique style of facial painting used by Alt, Beck & Gottschalck artists when I studied the shards and shoulder heads in a special display held in the Nauendorf Dorfmuseum in 1999. I visited the museum shortly after I toured the A.W. Fr. Kister porcelain factory in Scheibe-Alsbach. I toured the museum holding a large A.W. Fr. Kister glazed porcelain facial shard, which I compared with the shards and shoulder heads made by the Alt, Beck & Gottschalck porcelain factory in Nauendorf. I was surprised to see such a difference in facial painting. Alt, Beck & Gottschalck chinas and parian-like shoulder heads generally have a darker red lip line between the lips and outlined and highlighted irises. A.W. Fr. Kister chinas and parian-like shoulder heads do not have any of these facial painting characteristics.

The so-called Empress Eugenie 4-inch shoulder head pictured in illustration 7 on page 28 is typical of the earliest dolls made at the Nauendorf factory. The upper eyelids are outlined in black with the finest eyelid-definition lines imaginable. The eyebrows are multi-stroked. It is difficult to see the pale-blond eyebrow detail and the individual strokes of the well-painted eyelashes without a magnifying glass. The light-blue irises are outlined in a darker shade of blue. The black pupils are glazed. The light-red mouth has a slightly darker accent line between the upper and lower lips. The faces on some of the earliest shoulder heads are so smooth and shiny they appear to have been polished. The majority of

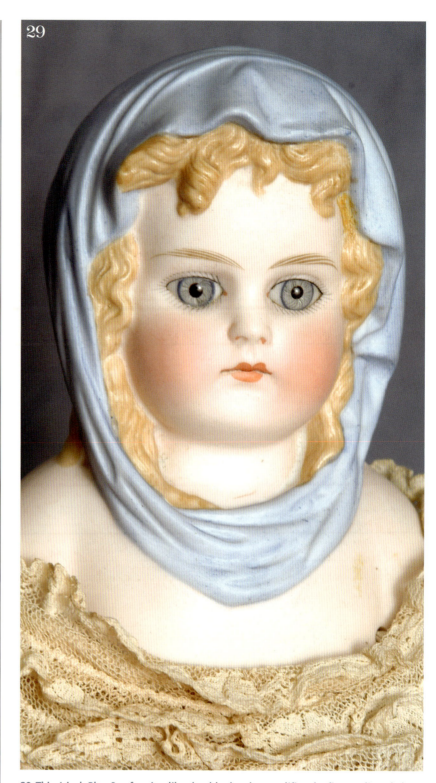

29. This 4-inch Blue Scarf parian-like shoulder head exemplifies the fine quality of Alt, Beck & Gottschalck doll-related porcelain products. The light-blue threaded irises add a touch of realism to the face. The multi-stroke eyebrows, upper and lower eyelashes and mouth with a darker-red lip accent line are finely painted. The molded curls extend out from the forehead. The shoulder-length hair is partially covered by a molded blue scarf that is draped over the shoulder plate in front. Eight wavy curls cover the neck in back. Margaret Hartshorn Collection. (Photo: Image Arts Etc.)

30. This 6½-inch shoulder head has typical factory facial features, which include blue painted eyes finely outlined in black, a tiny white iris highlight on the left side of each iris, and a V-shaped darker-red lip accent line. The shoulder plate is pierced below the neckline to hold a piece of coral. Susan Moore Collection. (Photo: Digital Images)

31. This 6-inch shoulder head was made from a master mold identical to the one used for the doll in illustration 30. The shoulder plate contains alternating cross-stitched and gathered bodice details. The upswept blond hair is styled in braids that encircle the head and form a semi-circle in front. An unusual pin is attached to the shoulder plate. Private Collection. (Photo: Estelle Johnston)

32. The back view of the shoulder head pictured in illustration 31 shows the molded braid and the vertical curls in varying lengths on the back of the head. Private Collection. (Photo: Estelle Johnston)

CHAPTER 2

33. This 4½-inch shoulder head has the same early style of facial painting found on the Empress Eugenies in illustrations 6 and 7. A three-strand gold bead necklace decorates the shoulder plate. The molded earrings are part of the mold, rather than a separate accessory. A gold-trimmed white feather fits into the circular holder on the top of the head. The facial features include multi-stroke eyebrows, vivid blue irises and upper and lower eyelashes. Terry Schmeltzer Collection. (Photo: Estelle Johnston)

34. A back view of the shoulder head in illustration 33 shows how the strands of gold beads define the separation between the large hair rolls. A gold comb holds the clustered curls in place on the nape of the neck. Terry Schmeltzer Collection. (Photo: Estelle Johnston)

35. This 4-inch shoulder head has blue glass eyes, upper and lower eyelashes and a darker line between the light-red lips and lobe-pierced exposed ears. The front hairstyle includes waves, a braid encircling the head and a black ribbon headband tied with an upside-down bow. The shoulder plate features a black ribbon necklace and a molded bodice decorated in a lace-like pattern. Margaret Hartshorn Collection. (Photo: Margaret Hartshorn)

36. The back view of the shoulder head in illustration 35 shows the large center braid and vertical curls of varying lengths on each side of the braid. Margaret Hartshorn Collection. (Photo: Margaret Hartshorn)

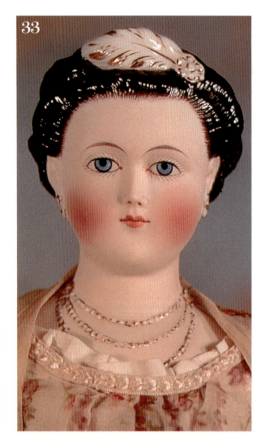
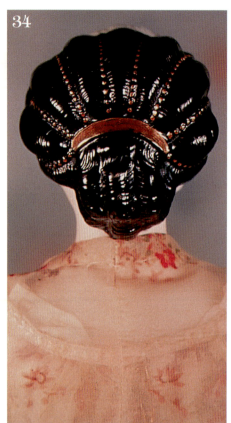

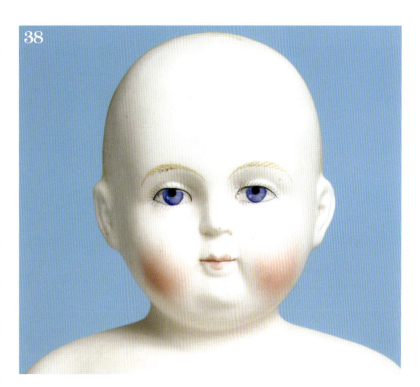

37. This early parian-like bald baby with a 3½-inch shoulder head has the same style of early facial painting as the dolls in illustrations 6 and 7. Finely painted brushstrokes soften the hairline on this unusual smooth bald head with black-painted hair. One difference between the baby's facial painting and the Empress Eugenie's painting in illustration 7 is its vivid, rather than light, blue irises. Terry Schmeltzer Collection. (Photo: Estelle Johnston)

38. This 4-inch early bald baby has pale-blond brush-marked hair (not visible in photo), multi-stroke eyebrows, upper and lower eyelashes and a darker-red lip accent line. An unusual painting feature is apparent on both this baby and the one in illustration 37: a pale-gray curved shadow line is painted from one side of the eye to the other, just below the pupil. This feature, often found on the earliest dolls, is also evident on the dolls in illustrations 7 and 8. Author's Collection. (Photo: Gregg Smith)

39. This 3½-inch shoulder head was made from a master mold similar to the one used for the shoulder head in illustration 33. This example has very smooth bisque and early facial painting. Features include multi-stroke eyebrows, exposed ears with molded earrings, vivid blue outlined irises, glazed pupils, upper and lower painted eyelashes and light-red lips with a darker-red accent line. Susan Moore Collection. (Photo: Digital Images)

40. This rare doll is wearing an original metal headband decorated with glass stones. The 5¼-inch shoulder head has blue glass eyes, upper and lower eyelashes, multi-stroke eyebrows and pierced ears. The ornate hairstyle is made up of braids, waves and puffs. Another special feature is the shoulder-plate decoration. Margaret Hartshorn Collection. (Photo: Image Arts Etc.)

41. The side view of the doll in illustration 40 shows the simulated diamond and amethyst tiara attached through holes pierced into the head. Margaret Hartshorn Collection. (Photo: Image Arts Etc.)

42. This 6-inch shoulder head has an upswept center-parted hairstyle with well-defined comb marks. The hair is held in place with a black comb trimmed with gold beads. The facial features on this well-modeled shoulder head are blue glass eyes, multi-stroke eyebrows, upper and lower eyelashes and a V-shaped darker-red lip accent line. A molded black ribbon, holding a white, gold-edged glazed pendant, encircles the neck. Private Collection. (Photo: Estelle Johnston)

43. A back view of the shoulder head in illustration 42 shows the elaborate arrangement of false hair attached to the back hairstyle, which includes a large bow and vertical curls. Private Collection. (Photo: Estelle Johnston)

40

1860s and 1870s heads painted at the factory differ from the earliest heads. On the later dolls, half-to three-quarters of the distance around each iris is outlined; and, the dark-red lip accent line is more pronounced. Also, the white iris highlights, painted on the left side of the iris only, are more easily seen.

We learn from the Ciesliks' *German Doll Encyclopedia* that, following the production of early shoulder heads, during the late 1880s the factory made: "Boy and girl heads with modeled hair, bonnets, hats or caps with painted eyes or glass eyes in 25 different sizes from 4 inches to 7.9 inches." From the book *Marks on German, Bohemian and Austrian Porcelain, 1710 to the Present* by Robert E. Röntgen, we also learn that the Alt, Beck & Gottschalck porcelain factory made "figurines, dolls, doll heads, decorative porcelain and religious articles from 1854 until 1953."

Exciting information about ABG production continues to surface. During the spring of 2005, Christiane Gräfnitz returned to Stützhaus on my behalf to take more photographs of the old porcelain factory in which both the ABG and Hertel, Schwab doll-related porcelain was made. The factory building is now in such poor condition that it is deemed unsafe to enter and is scheduled to be torn down in the near future. During Christiane's second trip to Stützhaus, Wolfgang Ortlepp gave her many more 1860s and 1870s shards and matching plaster working molds. Because of his generosity, identification of a large group of previously unknown Alt, Beck & Gottschalck glazed and unglazed porcelain shoulder heads with fancy hairstyles is now possible.

44. This 5-inch shoulder head with typical factory facial features and a finely modeled bodice is wearing a black molded necklace and cross pendant referred to as the German Iron Cross. A black headband decorated with gold beads holds the elaborate hairstyle in place. Doll collectors refer to this doll as Empress Augusta. Augusta Victoria was the wife of Kaiser Wilhelm II, grandson of Queen Victoria. Estelle Johnston Collection. (Photo: Estelle Johnston)

45. A back view of the shoulder head pictured in illustration 44 shows a mass of large comb-marked curls. Estelle Johnston Collection. (Photo: Estelle Johnston)

46. This 6-inch shoulder head has a molded bodice trimmed with a decorative necklace and a lightly glazed pink bow. This elaborate hairstyle was pictured in the July 8, 1871 issue of *Harpers Bazar* and described as the most popular hairstyle of the period. Olson/Nelson Collection. (Photo: Red Kite Studios)

47. The back hairstyle of the shoulder head shown in illustration 46 features braids and three large hair puffs banded with black ribbons. Olson/Nelson Collection. (Photo: Red Kite Studio)

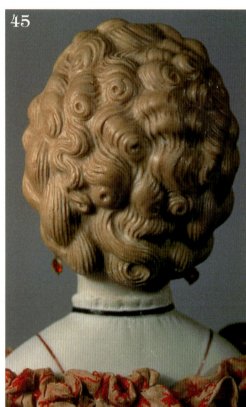

48. An 1870s braided hairstyle defines this lightly tinted 20-inch bisque shoulder head doll. The upswept hair is combed from a center part into two large coronet braids on top of the head. The bodice contains a tucked scalloped insert, gathered panels edged in dark-blue and blue shoulder bows. A black ribbon necklace holds a red simulated stone pendant. Private Collection. (Photo: Estelle Johnston)

49. The back hairstyle of the doll shown in illustration 48 features two separated sections of hair on the crown of the head, and large intertwined loops of hair molded on the nape of the neck. The ribbon necklace is tied in a bow on the back of the neck. Private Collection. (Photo: Estelle Johnston)

50. This 4¼-inch tinted shoulder head was made from a master mold identical to the one used for the doll in illustration 48. The black ribbon necklace holds a blue simulated stone pendant. Olson/Nelson Collection. (Photo: Red Kite Studios)

51. This 6-inch shoulder head has a short curly blond hairstyle and pierced ears. The neck ruffle on the bodice is decorated with a blue ribbon and a large blue shaded bow. Alt, Beck & Gottschalck shoulder heads with fancy hairstyles usually have single-stroke eyebrows, partially outlined irises and a white highlight on the left side of each iris. Olson/Nelson Collection. (Photo: Red Kite Studios)

52. This deeply tinted 4-inch 1890 bisque shoulder head is marked "1030 #4." The elaborate hairstyle is trimmed with black ribbons and forehead curls. The upper black ribbon band encircles the head and ends in a bow in the back. The white iris highlights look like tiny drops of white paint. Olson/Nelson Collection. (Photo: Red Kite Studios)

53. This 2½-inch 1890 parian-like shoulder head has deeply defined curls, blue glass eyes and pierced ears. The mouth painting includes the typical darker-red lip accent line seen on the majority of parian-like shoulder heads made by this factory. Courtesy Deutsches Spielzeugmuseum, Sonneberg. (Photo: Christiane Gräfnitz)

54. A white, gold-trimmed comb decorates the hair of this 5-inch shoulder head with an unusual asymmetrical upswept comb-marked hairstyle. The earring holes are pierced into the head. Olson/Nelson Collection. (Photo: Red Kite Studios)

55. The shoulder plate of the shoulder head shown in illustration 53 is incised with the mold number "1154" and the size number "11." The configuration of the number mark incised between the mold and size numbers is an excellent Alt, Beck & Gottschalck identification guide. The back hair is styled in what is commonly referred to as a French Twist. Courtesy Deutsches Spielzeugmuseum, Sonneberg. (Photo: Christiane Gräfnitz)

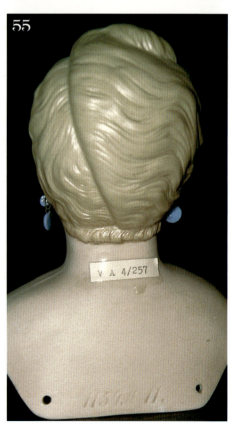

Alt, Beck & Gottschalck

56. This 4-inch shoulder head has unusual comb-marked bangs of varying lengths. A childlike look is created by the head modeling and facial painting. Kenneth Drew Collection. (Photo: Ann Hanat)

57. This 5½-inch shoulder head has short curly blond hair and a ruffled hat decorated with two separate blue ribbons and bows. The typical factory chubby cheeks and underarm indentations are easily visible on this doll. The shoulder plate of an identical head is marked with the 1890 mold number "1054." Kenneth Drew Collection. (Photo: Ann Hanat)

58. A light-blue bonnet trimmed with a darker-blue bow is a special feature on this 2½-inch shoulder head. The blond hairstyle includes bangs and long curls that spill onto the shoulders. Courtesy Deutsches Spielzeugmuseum, Sonneberg. (Photo: Christiane Gräfnitz)

59. The distinctive white headdress on this 3¾-inch shoulder head includes a double row of blue ruffles on top of the head and a scarf below. The draped head scarf continues on the shoulder plate. Courtesy Deutsches Spielzeugmuseum, Sonneberg. (Photo: Christiane Gräfnitz)

60. This bisque socket-head doll with boyish features is marked with intertwined fancy script ABG initials and an unreadable mold number. The side-parted hair complements the dimpled face. Glass eyes, multi-stroke eyebrows, upper and lower eyelashes and an open mouth with two upper teeth complete the appealing appearance of this 20-inch doll, circa 1920. Courtesy Deutsches Spielzeugmuseum, Sonneberg. (Photo: Christiane Gräfnitz)

61. Deeply defined comb-marked curls, dark multi-stroke eyebrows and large blue glass eyes are focal points on this 7-inch bisque shoulder head. Straight eyebrows are often found on bisque-head dolls made at the factory from the 1880s on. Kenneth Drew Collection. (Photo: Ann Hanat)

Chapter 3

C.F. Kling & Co.

1. The C.F. Kling porcelain factory is still standing in Ohrdruf today. Narrow gauge railroad tracks connect the factory buildings with the storage buildings. The tracks were used to transport raw materials in to, and finished products out of, the factory. (Photo: Mary Krombholz)

2. With the help of the Ohrdruf Town Museum curator Peter Cramer, Christiane Gräfnitz was able to make a clear copy of the Kling Anniversary showcase photograph on display in the museum. Courtesy Ohrdruf Town Museum.

One C.F. Kling & Co. porcelain factory building is still standing in the Thuringian town of Ohrdruf, which has a population of about 6,500. The old factory building is in very poor condition. Weeds partially cover the narrow-gauge railroad that once transported raw materials and finished products in and out of the factory. The historic inn, Zum Deutchen Hof, located across the street from the factory, was used as a factory warehouse beginning in 1867. The original main doorway features large molded birds and an ornate crown. The earliest medallion attached to the building is dated 1808.

Examples of parian-like Kling shoulder heads are found in an old photograph in the permanent collection of the Ohrdruf Town Museum. The photograph is of a large C. F. Kling & Co. showcase that once contained examples of one hundred years of the factory's porcelain production. The showcase was featured at the 1934 Leipzig Fair to commemorate the 100th Anniversary Leipzig Fair visit of the Kling factory. A large oval sign attached to the showcase contains the following German words: "1834 (Kling trademark) 1934; 100 Jahre Messebesuch; Der Firma; C. F. Kling & Co.; Ohrdruf/Thur.; Zimmer 335 Aufg. D." The English translation is "1834-1934; 100 Year Fair Visit; For The C.F. Kling & Co.; Ohrdruf, Thuringia; Room 335 Hall D." The German letters Aufg are the contraction of the German word Aufgang, which means hall.

Chapter 3

3. An enlargement of the showcase photo shows the distinctive parian-like shoulder heads on the lower shelf, which are in doll collections all over the world. The six shoulder heads circled were made from master molds identical to those used for Kling parian-like dolls currently in American doll collections and shown in this book in the following illustrations, from left: 59, 28, 24, 4, 5, 41. I am grateful to the collectors who generously shared their Kling "showcase" dolls with the readers of this book. Courtesy Ohrdruf Town Museum.

This important photograph is enlarged to show the parian-like shoulder heads displayed on the bottom shelf of the showcase. Six shoulder heads made from identical master molds are currently owned by three American doll collectors. Shown in this chapter (illustrations 4, 5, 24, 28, 41 and 59), these shoulder heads show the outstanding modeling and painting details created by factory employees during the 1860s and 1870s.

The showcase is described in detail in the August 4, 1937, issue of *Thüringen Waldbote* (Wood Herald/Messenger) in an article titled: "100 Years of Ohrdruf Porcelain." The description of the showcase is as follows: "One of the rooms at the city museum is dedicated to the present. There are exhibits of two of the important companies in our city. The wide window front of the room is taken up by two showcases and an open cabinet by the C.F. Kling Company, which celebrated their 100th

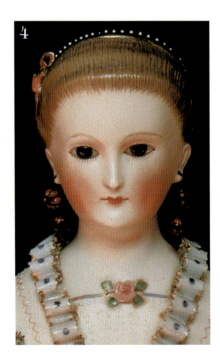

4. A study of the Kling 100th Anniversary showcase reveals an unusual 4¾-inch shoulder head made from a master mold identical to the one used for this shoulder head. Applied porcelain ruffles form a "V" on the molded bodice. Facial features include blue glass eyes, tan multi-stroke eyebrows, upper and lower eyelashes and pierced ears. A molded rose, leaves and embroidery decorate the bodice inside the ruffled porcelain collar. Margaret Hartshorn Collection. (Photo: Image Arts Etc)

C.F. Kling & Co.

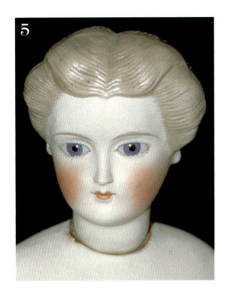
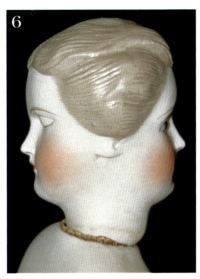

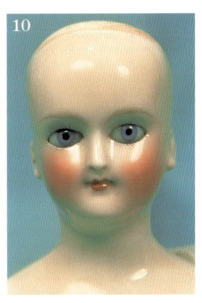

5. This 1860s two-faced Kling with a 4½-inch shoulder head and a swivel neck is currently on display in the Ohrdruf Town Museum. It was made from a master mold identical to the one used for the two-faced Kling pictured on the right side of the Kling Anniversary showcase, seen in illustration 3. The head features light gray/brown hair, glass eyes, multi-stroke eyebrows, upper and lower eyelashes and a well-painted mouth. Courtesy Ohrdruf Town Museum. (Photo: Christiane Gräfnitz)

6. The side view of the doll in illustration 5 shows the hair modeling that joins the two faces. Courtesy Ohrdruf Town Museum. (Photo: Christiane Gräfnitz)

7. The sleeping face of the doll in illustration 5 has closed eyes with molded eyelids featuring long painted eyelashes. The hairstyles are the same on both sides of the head. Courtesy Ohrdruf Town Museum. (Photo: Christiane Gräfnitz)

8. The back of the head pictured in illustration 9 shows the flared twisted hair that encircles the head. A large hair puff is modeled in the center of the long straight hair. The shoulder plate is marked with the Kling number and "4W6." Courtesy Deutsches Spielzeugmuseum, Sonneberg. (Photo: Christiane Gräfnitz)

9. A 5-inch early Kling shoulder head has similar facial modeling as the glazed porcelain shoulder head shown in illustration 10. The blond center-parted hairstyle with well-defined comb marks contains a large coronet-type braid. The head features blue glass eyes, multi-stroke eyebrows and upper and lower eyelashes. Courtesy Deutsches Spielzegmuseum, Sonneberg. (Photo: Christiane Gräfnitz)

10. This 3½-inch glazed porcelain shoulder head has a bald head, bright blue glass eyes, small flat ears and a closed mouth. The facial modeling and painting of this china is identical to the modeling and painting on many early parian-like dolls made by the Kling porcelain factory. Because existing original factory records do not describe the production of specific shoulder heads, it is difficult to document the first porcelain shoulder heads made by this factory. Susan Moore Collection. (Photo: Frank McAloon)

Chapter 3

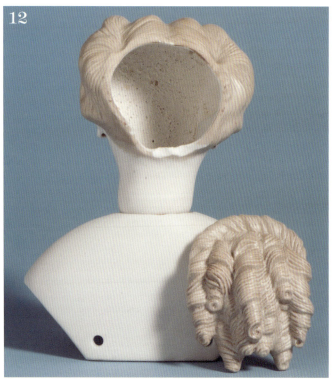

11. This 5-inch parian-like shoulder head has a swivel neck. The separate shoulder plate is identical to the shape of the shoulder plates shown in illustrations 7 and 9. The café-au-lait upswept hairstyle includes waves on each side of a center part. The earliest Kling parian-like shoulder heads often have flared ear lobes and an indentation on the outside edges of the ears. Author's Collection. (Photo: Gregg Smith)

12. The back view of the shoulder head in illustration 11 shows the head opening and the removable cluster of curls. Author's Collection. (Photo: Gregg Smith)

13. The back view of the hairstyle of the shoulder head pictured in illustration 14 shows another special feature of this shoulder head. Applied roses and leaves decorate the hair above the fixed cluster of curls. Estelle Johnston Collection. (Photo: Estelle Johnston)

14. This 4-inch shoulder head, made from a master mold identical to the one used for the shoulder head in illustration 11 has glass eyes and a rare open mouth with a molded tongue tip. The hairstyle includes fine brushstrokes around the hairline and waved comb-marked hair arranged on each side of a center part. Estelle Johnston Collection. (Photo: Estelle Johnston)

C.F. Kling & Co.

CHAPTER 3

15

This shoulder head, made from an identical mold as the dolls in illustrations 4, 16 and 18, differs in some aspects. The hair on this shoulder head is painted the same color as the dolls pictured in illustrations 4 and 16. The biggest difference is in the painting of the shoulder plate and applied ruching. The doll in illustration 4 has a molded rose in the center of the bodice, while the doll in illustration 16 has a white bead necklace around her neck. This example features elaborate hand-painted scrolls that cover the shoulder plate. Estelle Johnston Collection. (Photo: Estelle Johnston)

C.F. Kling & Co.

16. This 4¾-inch shoulder head was made from a master mold identical to the one used for the shoulder head in illustrations 4 and 15. It differs only in that the applied V-shaped ruffled porcelain collar is painted in different colors and the painted rickrack pattern varies in width. A white bead molded necklace decorates the bodice, rather than a molded rose. Olson/Nelson Collection. (Photo: Red Kite Studios)

17. The back view of the shoulder head in illustration 16 shows the molded pink bow on the right side of the head. The comb-marked hairstyle features rolls of hair encircling the head and two raised hair puffs in the middle. Olson/Nelson Collection. (Photo: Red Kite Studios)

18. Another example of a shoulder head with black hair is made from a master mold identical to the one used for the shoulder heads in illustrations 4, 15 and 16. It is in the collection of the Sonneberg Doll Museum. Courtesy Deutsches Spielzeugmuseum, Sonneberg. (Photo: Christiane Gräfnitz)

19. The profile of the 4-inch black-haired shoulder head in illustration 18 shows the decorated headband and bow that vary in color from the other examples made from the same mold. Courtesy Deutsches Spielzeugmuseum. (Photo: Christiane Gräfnitz)

20. A large black gold-trimmed comb decorates the elaborate hairstyle on this elegant lady doll with a 5½-inch shoulder head. The ornate shoulder plate is decorated with molded ruffles inside a wide gold-trimmed collar. The typical pink and blue Kling colors were used to paint the applied porcelain ruffle, bow and intricate shoulder plate design. Olson/Nelson Collection. (Photo: Red Kite Studios)

21. The back view of the hairstyle seen in illustration 20 shows the large braid encircling the crown-like comb. Two separate sections of applied ruching are a continuation of the front shoulder-plate detail. The back shoulder plate is marked with the typical Kling number and letter combination "5K7." Olson/Nelson Collection. (Photo: Red Kite Studios)

22. This 5-inch parian-like shoulder head has a hairstyle identical to the one on the shoulder head in illustrations 20 and 21. The applied collar, porcelain ruffle and painted shoulder-plate details differ. Estelle Johnston Collection. (Photo: Estelle Johnston)

23. Shades of Kling pink were used to paint the elaborate design on the double row of V-shaped ruffled porcelain on this shoulder head in the Sonneberg Doll Museum. A molded rose with green leaves decorates the hair between the two hair puffs on top of the head. A row of tightly wound curls is molded across the forehead. Note the similarity of these forehead curls to the curls in the 1867 fashion illustration shown in the Introduction. Courtesy Deutsches Spielzeugmuseum, Sonneberg. (Photo: Christiane Gräfnitz)

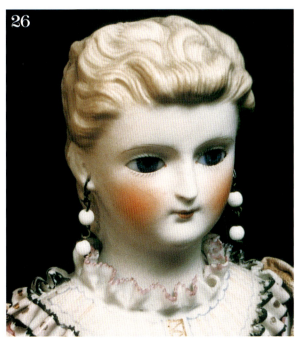

24. Talented Kling modelers and artists created this breathtaking 5-inch shoulder head wearing an ornate blue and gold necklace with an oval pendant. A shoulder head made from an identical master mold is in the Kling 100th Anniversary showcase. The hairstyle features a braid across the top of the head and a strand of gold beads applied over the tiny curls on the forehead. The hand-painted details on the shoulder plate are identical in color to many Kling shoulder plates shown in this chapter. Estelle Johnston Collection. (Photo: Estelle Johnston)

25. A molded braid encircles the head of the shoulder head shown in illustration 24. Long vertical curls partially cover the gold necklace and end above the painted shoulder-plate detail. Estelle Johnston Collection. (Photo: Estelle Johnston)

26. This 4-inch shoulder head has pierced ears, blue glass eyes with realistic threading, upper and lower painted eyelashes and multi-stroke eyebrows. The attached shoulder plate is decorated with applied oval-shaped ruching and a high ruffled collar. The shoulder plate is painted in pink, black and gold designs. The tan-colored upswept hair is waved in front and includes vertical curls that end on the collar in back. Margaret Hartshorn Collection. (Photo: Margaret Hartshorn)

Chapter 3

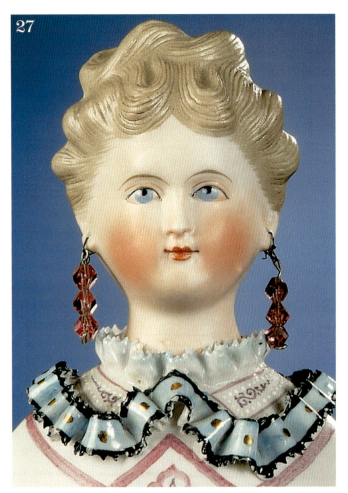

27. This 4-inch parian-like shoulder head with a decorated shoulder plate is painted with the Kling colors identical to those found on many shoulder heads in this chapter. The elaborate decorations include a high ruffled collar and applied scalloped ruching bordered by hand painted details. Olson/Nelson Collection. (Photo: Red Kite Studios)

28. This rare 3½-inch shoulder head was made from a master mold identical to the one used for a shoulder head located in the center of the front row on the lower shelf of the Kling Anniversary showcase. This shoulder head wears the same distinctive Scottish Tam as the shoulder head in the showcase. The top of the hat is painted in a plaid pattern. The hatband, featuring a molded feather, is painted in a pink and black checkerboard pattern. The original factory body includes laced boots painted in the same plaid pattern as the Tam. A molded gold-edged collar and a polka-dot tie decorate the shoulder plate. The head has pierced earrings, blue glass eyes, multi-stroke eyebrows, upper and lower eyelashes and a typical long narrow nose. The long curly blond hairstyle is molded on one side of the shoulder plate in front. Margaret Hartshorn Collection. (Photo: Image Arts Etc)

29. The plaid and checkerboard designs are focal points on the unusual molded hat worn by the shoulder head in illustration 28. The long molded hair covers a large portion of the shoulder plate in back. Margaret Hartshorn Collection. (Photo: Image Arts Etc.)

30. A shoulder head made from a master mold similar to the one used for the example shown in illustration 31 has a smaller V-shaped painted design under the shoulder plate's molded ruffle and beads. Susan Moore Collection. (Photo: Digital Images)

31. Pink molded roses and green leaves decorate the circle braid molded over the forehead on this 5-inch shoulder head with lobe-pierced ears and typical factory facial painting details. The back hairstyle features looped braids. Olson/Nelson Collection. (Photo: Red Kite Studios)

32. The back hair of the shoulder head seen in illustration 30 contains an unusual arrangement of molded braids. Susan Moore Collection. (Photo: Digital Images)

anniversary. The production of doll heads has been the biggest part of their production. Therefore, one of the showcases was taken up mostly by doll heads. They show the changing tastes over this past century in foreign countries as well as within this country. In the middle we see big vases and colorful lively looking figurines of ladies and gentlemen.

"The following can be reported about the old company, well-known all over Germany and many foreign countries. The founder of the company was Christian Friedrich Kling. In 1834, he had his first exhibit at the Leipzig Fall Show. In August 1837 he finally founded the company. Back then, they mainly made figurines, reliefs and vases. At the end of the 1850s, they started the production of household dishes. Soon, this was abandoned and the company started to make porcelain dolls, dollhouse dolls and children figurines only. It was those items that gave the company its worldwide reputation. The export of the items worldwide was very important."

This historic information from the *Thüringen Waldbote* is extremely important because it documents, for the first time, the early 1860s production of shoulder heads. And it is especially important for doll collectors to know that, during this time period, the factory made "porcelain dolls, dollhouse dolls and children figurines only." From this sentence we learn that the factory made large numbers of porcelain dolls,

Chapter 3

33. This 4-inch parian-like shoulder head, circa 1860s, has tight clusters of small curls on each side of a glazed applied bow on top of the head. The head features include glass eyes, multi-stroke eyebrows, upper and lower eyelashes and pierced ears. The ornate shoulder plate is decorated with a square-necked applied porcelain ruffle bordered by gold beads. Terry Schmeltzer Collection. (Photo: Estelle Johnston)

34. The applied bow with streamers, ruffle and gold beads are seen in the back view of the shoulder head in illustration 33. Terry Schmeltzer Collection. (Photo: Estelle Johnston)

35. Forehead curls, a molded bow painted the same color as the hair and a brush-marked upswept hairstyle define this 12-inch parian-like doll known as Countess Dagmar. Its walking mechanism was patented in 1862. The "jewel" eyes, which have convex eyeballs that extend beyond the molded upper and lower eyelids, are a very unusual modeled facial feature. The large round pupils and white lines radiating around the blue irises create very lifelike eyes that look like glass eyes in a photograph. Estelle Johnston Collection. (Photo: Estelle Johnston)

36. The back view of the doll in illustration 35 shows the smooth comb-marked section of hair and hair rolls held in place with molded braids. Private Collection. (Photo: Estelle Johnston)

C.F. Kling & Co.

37

This 4-inch parian-like shoulder head has applied gold-edged blue ribbon bows over each ear. A matching bow with long streamers adds interest to the top of the head. Note the arrangement of the clustered curls across the forehead. Estelle Johnston Collection. (Photo: Estelle Johnston)

38. This 6½-inch shoulder head was made from a master mold similar to the one used for the doll in illustration 35. Both examples have molded bows painted the same color as the hair. On this example, the buttons on the molded high-necked bodice are unpainted. Olson/Nelson Collection. (Photo: Red Kite Studios)

39. A slightly different version of the Countess Dagmar hairstyle shown in illustrations 35 and 38 features a cluster of curls molded on the forehead and a ribbed headband painted the same color as the hair. A wide gold-trimmed black comb holds the large cluster of curls in back. Note the flared earlobes and indentations on the outer edges of the ears. Olson/Nelson Collection. (Photo: Red Kite Studios)

40. This black-haired 4½-inch Countess Dagmar has painted brown eyes, brush-marked hair and a large molded comb holding a cluster of curls molded on the nape of the neck. Olson/Nelson Collection. (Photo: Red Kite Studios)

C.F. Kling & Co.

41. A distinctive 4¾-inch shoulder head is on the far right of the Kling 100th Anniversary showcase, in illustration 3. The hairstyle includes masses of tightly wound curls with deeply indented ends. Kling molded curls often have holes molded into the end of each curl. A molded spray of large pink roses and green leaves edged in gold adorns the café-au-lait hair. The back hairstyle includes a smooth comb-marked center section and masses of curls identical to those on the front. The 4¾-inch shoulder head has lobe pierced ears, single-stroke eyebrows, blue painted eyes and a white highlight on the left side of each iris. The modeling and facial painting on the showcase shoulder head are identical to this doll's. Olson/Nelson Collection. (Photo: Red Kite Studios)

42. This Countess Dagmar has a black headband partially covered by a cluster of forehead curls. Note the similarity of the facial painting on all the Kling parian-like shoulder heads made in the 1860s. Margaret Hartshorn Collection. (Photo: Image Arts Etc.)

presumably parian-like dolls similar to the shoulder heads found in the 100th Anniversary Showcase.

We also learn from the *Thüringen Waldbote* the following history: "Several years before his death in 1870, the founder of the Chr. Fr. Kling & Co. company passed the leadership on to his two oldest sons Ernst Friedrich Kling and Otto. Otto soon passed away. Ernst Friedrich Kling led the porcelain factory until his death in 1878. His son Paul Kling took over the company at the young age of 21. He asked his uncle Louis Ortlepp to be his assistant. Unfortunately, Paul died only eleven years after being the head of the company. He had built the steam driven Masse mill in the factory court yard in Ohrdruf, as well as central heating for all fabrication rooms."

In his book *History of Gotha Cities*, author A. Beck also provides a detailed history of the C.F. Kling & Co. porcelain factory. One paragraph describes the three Kling porcelain factories in the following way: "The first porcelain factory founded by C.F. Kling in 1837 was very successful. In 1867 they changed the

CHAPTER 3

43. This 6-inch Kling shoulder head was made from a master mold identical to the one used for the doll in illustration 44. The painting colors and details on the shoulder plate vary considerably. Author's Collection. (Photo: Red Kite Studios)

44. The typical Kling shades of pink and blue are very evident on the shoulder plate of this shoulder head with hair puffs arranged on each side of a center part. Olson/Nelson Collection. (Photo: Red Kite Studios)

45. Additional hair puffs and vertical curls in varying lengths decorate the back of the head. The number "9" is incised on the back shoulder plate. Olson/Nelson Collection. (Photo: Red Kite Studios)

old inn 'Zum Deutschen Hof' into a new warehouse. In 1859, they opened a second factory (the Kästner factory). In 1863, they opened a third porcelain factory. It was the Steuding factory, which was below Stützhaus in the city area. Those factories were combined with toy stores and employed more than 1200 people."

The following number and letter combinations have been found on the back shoulder plates of early C.F. Kling & Co. parian-like heads: 2K3, 3S3, 4B5, 4N9, 4P9, 4R7, 4W0, 5Y6, 3L5, 5A5, 5B5, 5C5, 5H5, 5M5 5U2, 5V2 and 5Y6. The facial modeling and the facial painting details on

66

C.F. Kling & Co.

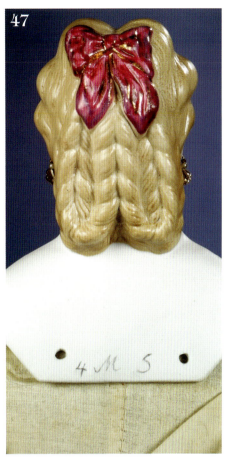

46. This 4½-inch shoulder head has an unusual blond hairstyle with two large hair puffs and two smaller hair puffs arranged on each side of a center part. The shoulder plate decorations include a stand-up collar with pointed ends partially covering a porcelain ruffle. The knotted white scarf is painted with the typical factory blue and deep-pink polka dots. Olson/Nelson Collection. (Photo: Red Kite Studios)

47. A large magenta bow decorates the back hairstyle on this shoulder plate. Two large looped braids are molded onto the shoulders. The shoulder plate is marked with the Kling letter and number combination "4M5." Olson/Nelson Collection. (Photo: Red Kite Studios)

48. This 3¼-inch shoulder head with a side-parted hairstyle has horizontal curls deeply indented on the ends. The molded shirt, gold-trimmed high collar and tie are well modeled. This shoulder head was named Dresden Gent by doll collectors. The cloth body on a shoulder head made from an identical master mold was marked with the name and address of C.W. Leipold. According to *The Collector's Encyclopedia of Dolls, Volume I*, by Dorothy, Elizabeth Ann and Evelyn Jane Coleman, Leipold was listed in New York directories in 1867 and 1868. Susan Moore Collection. (Photo: Digital Images)

49. The collar painting on the pleated shirt worn by this 6-inch shoulder head varies slightly from that on the doll in illustration 48, which was made from an identical master mold. One molded tie is painted in a striped pattern while the other is painted in a polka dot pattern. Olson/Nelson Collection. (Photo: Red Kite Studios)

CHAPTER 3

52. This 3½-inch shoulder head with a slightly different glazed hairstyle shows the shape of the shoulder plates found on many Kling dolls made in the 1860s and 1870s. Author's Collection. (Photo: Red Kite Studios)

50. This 6-inch shoulder head with a black hairstyle varies from the Kling center-parted glazed hairstyle pictured in illustrations 53, 58, 59, 60, 62, 63 and 64. The hairstyle is decorated with molded flowers, leaves and a decorative scarf. Large pink roses, small white bell-shaped flowers and white, pink-veined leaves are arranged in front of the blue twisted glazed scarf. Olson/Nelson Collection. (Photo: Red Kite Studios)

51. The back of the shoulder head pictured in illustration 50 shows the glazed black comb-marked hair with a smooth crown twisted into a chignon on the nape of the neck. The blue glazed scarf is trimmed in white. Olson/Nelson Collection. (Photo: Red Kite Studios)

53. A strand of beads painted the same color as the hair adds interest to this 3¼-inch shoulder head with a similar center parted hairstyle as the doll in illustration 63. Olson/Nelson Collection. (Photo: Red Kite Studios)

54. This rare 4½-inch shoulder head has a blond center-parted hairstyle featuring two large gold barrettes. The molded details on the shoulder plate are similar to the Kling with the bald head shown in illustration 67, except that this shoulder head has a pink bow with gold-painted trim. Estelle Johnston Collection. (Photo: Estelle Johnston)

55. This uncommon 4-inch shoulder head has a high collar trimmed with a wide ribbon and bow painted in the two shades of pink often used by Kling factory artists. The upswept hairstyle is decorated with a black gold-trimmed headband woven through the blond hair. A three-strand gold necklace with an attached pendant is molded inside the unusual collar. Margaret Hartshorn Collection. (Photo: Margaret Hartshorn)

56. The shoulder head on this 18-inch blond-haired doll was made from a master mold similar to the one used for the shoulder head in illustration 50, although the applied decorations vary slightly. The molded scarf, flowers and leaves are pictured and described in the book *Dolls of Yesterday* by Eleanor St. George. The doll, which once belonged to Miss Alma Roebuck, is pictured in an illustration following page 92. Private Collection. (Photo: Estelle Johnston)

57. A back view shows the hairstyle differences between this example and the shoulder head in illustration 51. The molded scarf is longer and the hairstyle is less flared. PrivateCollection. (Photo: Estelle Johnston)

58. This 4½-inch shoulder head with a similar flared hairstyle as the doll in illustration 64 has pierced ears and a black-trimmed ruffle holding the snood in back. The molded blouse features a large blue applied bow instead of a striped tie. Olson/Nelson Collection. (Photo: Red Kite Studios)

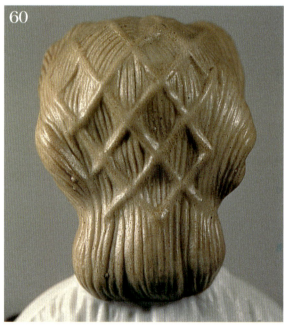

59. This 3½-inch shoulder head has a similar hairstyle and shoulder plate decoration as the shoulder heads shown in illustrations 58, 62, 63 and 64. The collar and blue-striped tie are generously edged and trimmed in gold. Estelle Johnston Collection. (Photo: Estelle Johnston)

60. The back of the hair of the shoulder head in illustration 59 shows the long comb-marked hairstyle and lattice-like molded snood, which is painted the same color as the hair. The molded bodice is gathered on the front and back. Estelle Johnston Collection. (Photo: Estelle Johnston)

the marked Klings pictured in this chapter are identical to several of the shoulder heads in the Kling Anniversary showcase photograph.

Two early C.F. Kling & Co. parian-like shoulder heads are pictured on page 77 of the Colemans' book *The Collector's Encyclopedia of Dolls*. A shoulder head made from an identical master mold is pictured in this book, in illustration 11 on page 54. A similar shoulder head, in the collection of the Museum of the City of New York, is pictured on page 40 of John Noble's 1967 book, *Dolls*, and an example identical to those on pages 77 and 87 in the Colemans' book, with an open mouth and molded teeth, is also pictured on page 40 of Noble's book.

C.F. Kling & Co.

61. This black-haired doll has well-painted details on the collar and tie. Note the difference in the hand painting on the tie as compared to that on the dolls pictured in illustrations 59, 62, 63, 65 and 66. Estelle Johnston Collection. (Photo: Estelle Johnston)

62. This 4¾-inch shoulder head was made from a master mold identical to the one used for the shoulder head pictured on the left side of the Kling Anniversary showcase, seen in illustration 3. The long blond wavy hairstyle is flared on each side of the center part. The original gold paint is barely visible on this decorated shoulder plate featuring a collar and blue striped tie with notched ends. A molded snood holds the back hair in back. Olson/Nelson Collection. (Photo: Red Kite Studios)

63. This 4½-inch shoulder head made from a master mold identical to the one used for the shoulder head in illustration 62 has black hair and similar shoulder plate decorations. The hair is combed back from the face into loose curls. A snood decorates the hair in back. Olson/Nelson Collection. (Photo: Red Kite Studios)

64. A close view of a 5-inch Kling shoulder head made from a master mold identical to the one used for the dolls in illustrations 62 and 63 shows its glazed hairstyle, white iris highlights and molded collar and tie. An important identification guide is the heart-like shape of Kling painted mouths. Thin, slightly curved lines extend between the upper and lower lips. The lip line is painted the same color as the lips. Author's Collection. (Photo: Gregg Smith)

CHAPTER 3

65. This 5½-inch shoulder head has a similar collar and tie as the lady dolls shown in illustrations 59, 62 and 63. The full face contrasts with the long oval face shapes of the lady dolls, although the gathered bodice molded on the shoulder plate is similar. Olson/Nelson Collection. (Photo: Red Kite Studios)

66. A 4-inch shoulder head with a slimmer face than the doll in illustration 65 has a similar center-parted hairstyle and decorated shoulder plate. Olson/Nelson Collection. (Photo: Red Kite Studios)

67. This 4¾-inch bald head Kling has shoulder plate modeling similar to many of the shoulder heads pictured in this chapter, although it is lacking a collar and tie. Courtesy Ohrdruf Town Museum. (Photo: Christiane Gräfnitz)

Another documentation of this early C.F. Kling & Co. shoulder head with a removable cluster of molded curls, is in the book entitled *The Rose Unfolds* by Rosalie Whyel and Susan Hedrick. The doll is on permanent display in the Rosalie Whyel Doll Museum in Bellevue, Washington. The authors provide important information on the American distributor of the doll in the following way: "Her head is one of a group imported in the late 19th century by the U.S. based company of George Borgfeldt. It is illustrated in Colemans' *Encyclopedia of Dolls* (vol. 1, p. 77) as part of a group donated to the Museum of the City of New York by Fred Kolb, a former president of the Borgfeldt Company. The Colemans have studied Fred Kolb's encoded documentation that came with these doll heads, and feel that this fine example was made by the German firm, Kling."

For many years, many Kling parian-like shoulder heads have been wrongly attributed to the Dornheim, Koch & Fischer porcelain factory. Christiane Gräfnitz visited Gräfenroda in March 2004 to learn more about the porcelain factory for this book. After talking to the town mayor (a former porcelain-factory worker) and other former factory workers, Christiane began to question the research indicating the Gräfenroda factory made doll-related porcelain in the 1860s and 1870s.

The dated entries of the *Gräfenroda Chronicles* provide important dates relating to the history of the town, beginning with the first written

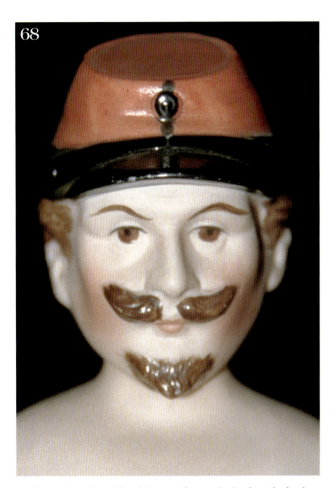

68. The #303-2/0 mold and size number are incised on the back shoulder plate of this Kling man. According to the Ciesliks' *German Doll Marks and Identification Book*, the #303 was made circa 1897. The 3½-inch shoulder head is wearing a red molded hat with a small black brim. Courtesy Ohrdruf Town Museum. (Photo: Christiane Gräfnitz)

69. While similar to the shoulder head in illustration 68, this circa-1897 Kling man has a smaller molded mustache and goatee and wears a differently styled molded hat. The black hat is trimmed in orange and yellow. This 3½-inch shoulder head is marked "#305-2/0." Courtesy Ohrdruf Museum. (Photo: Christiane Gräfnitz)

records of the town's name in 1290. In an entry from 1880, the historical document dates the founding of the Dornheim, Koch & Fischer porcelain factory. From the *Chronicles* we learn: "Mr. Koch, Mr. Fischer Senior and Junior from Plaue, and earthen ware manufacturer Heinrich Dornheim came together to found a porcelain factory." This entry proves that the large group of parian-like shoulder heads with 1860s and 1870s elaborate hairstyles and shoulder plates were made by the C.F. Kling rather than the Dornheim, Koch & Fischer porcelain factory. The shoulder heads in the Kling 100th Anniversary showcase also offer definitive proof that a very distinctive group of parian-like "fancies" was made in the Kling factory.

Author Robert E. Röntgen lists the porcelain products made by the Dornheim, Koch & Fischer porcelain factory in his book titled *Marks on German, Bohemian and Austrian Porcelain, 1710 to the Present*. Doll heads are not listed as products of the porcelain factory. Röntgen lists the products as: "decorative porcelain, figurines and gift articles." They were made from the 1880 founding of the factory until the factory closed in 1938. Röntgen lists the products of the C.F. Kling & Co. porcelain factory, circa 1837-1951, as: "dolls and dolls' heads, figurines."

Antique-doll collectors avidly collect the ornate parian-like shoulder heads made by the Kling porcelain factory. Hairstyles include molded hair curls, puffs, rolls, braids and chignons. The hair is trimmed with molded flowers in the Dresden manner, as well as with beads, combs, barrettes, hair bands and ribbons. The resemblance to the porcelain figurines and vases normally described as Dresden is unmistakable. For many years, American doll collectors believed these elaborate shoulder heads were made in Dresden, Germany. We now

CHAPTER 3

70. A gray hat with a black trimmed brim is worn by this circa-1885 childlike Kling. The 4-inch shoulder head is marked "160-5." The head has blue glass eyes, multi-stroke eyebrows and upper and lower eyelashes. The unusual open/closed mouth has painted teeth. The shoulder plate decorations include a V-shaped ruffled porcelain collar and the same type of flat painted details found on earlier parian-like dolls made by this factory. Margaret Hartshorn Collection. (Photo: Image Arts Etc.)

71. This 4-inch shoulder head features a molded hat with a black band and long gold-trimmed streamers molded on one shoulder. The front shoulder plate contains a gold-trimmed collar and blue shaded bow. The back shoulder plate is marked with the 1880 mold number "116." Margaret Hartshorn Collection. (Photo: Margaret Hartshorn)

72. This unusual 6-inch Kling shoulder head is in the permanent collection of the Sonneberg Doll Museum. The gray molded hat is decorated with a black molded hatband, a gold-and-white circular medallion and a glazed feather. A blue molded bow trims the unusual braided necklace. Courtesy Deutsches Spielzeugmuseum, Sonneberg. (Photo: Christiane Gräfnitz)

know the majority were made by the C.F. Kling & Co. porcelain factory.

Janet Johl describes Dresden shoulder heads in her 1941 book titled *The Fascinating Story of Dolls*. Johl states: "The influence of Dresden is seen in the extensive use of molded patterns, flowers, ornaments and gilt relief raised from the flat ground of the dead white porcelain." In Johl's 1946 book, *More About Dolls*, she continues her description of Dresden doll heads as follows: "The city of Dresden, Germany, which was engaged in true porcelain making as early as 1709, turned out some lovely Parian pieces. In dolls, the heads were often decorated with wreaths of miniature glazed flowers, or with a gold luster hair ornament; a band of black satin, shiny ribbon, or a gilt net snood."

Like Janet Johl, Eleanor St. George contributed an important body of research for doll collectors to learn from today. St. George accurately documented antique dolls through oral histories given by original

C.F. Kling & Co.

73. This 4½-inch shoulder head was made from a master mold identical to the one used to make the doll in illustration 74, but its details are slightly different. The applied hair bow is not exactly the same and the applied ruffled collar is oval in shape rather than squared off at the corners. Many details on parian-like shoulder plates made from identical master molds vary because they were applied by hand. This shoulder head lacks the glass eyes, multi-stroke eyebrows and upper and lower eyelashes seen on the shoulder head in illustration 74. Olson/Nelson Collection. (Photo: Red Kite Studios)

owners. The St. George 1948 book, *Dolls of Yesterday*, includes a photograph of a C.F. Kling & Co. parian-like shoulder head doll in the section of illustrations following page 92. The author states: "The collector who has firsthand information on the history of a Dresden parian head is Miss Alma Robeck. Miss Robeck's great grandfather came from Germany in the 1850s and conducted a confectionary and bakery business in Annapolis. Every Christmas he sent to Germany for various novelties for his Christmas trade. Among these were a number of Dresden Parian doll heads. One of these heads was bought by an Annapolis family. When the old lady

74. This childlike Kling has a decorated 1870s-type hairstyle with accentuated hair height on the crown of the head. The front hair is decorated with a large black molded bow. The head features include pierced ears, blue glass eyes, multi-stroke eyebrows and upper and lower painted eyelashes. The ruffled porcelain collar and shoulder plate are painted with the typical Kling deep-pink and blue colors. Terry Schmeltzer Collection. (Photo: Estelle Johnston)

75. The hairstyle on this 5-inch shoulder head is unusual because it has a brightly painted bird attached to the coronet-like braids. The center-parted hairstyle is styled in waves. Courtesy Deutches Spielzeugmuseum, Sonneberg. (Photo: Christiane Gräfnitz)

76. A rear view of the shoulder head in illustration 75 shows two large vertical braids covering the center of the head. The shoulder plate is marked with the Kling mold and size number combination "118-6," circa 1880. A childlike face and a differently sculpted shoulder plate define this later parian-like shoulder head. Courtesy Deutsches Spielzeugmuseum, Sonneberg. (Photo: Christiane Gräfnitz)

Chapter 3

77. This childlike Kling with a 4¾-inch shoulder head has a turned, downward-looking head and pierced ears. The center-parted hair is styled with a large coronet braid and flat forehead curls. Loosely formed vertical curls decorate the back hairstyle. Note the generous cheek blushing and open/closed mouth with painted teeth. The upper lip is painted with the typical Kling downward line. Olson/Nelson Collection. (Photo: Red Kite Studios)

78. This 10-inch bisque Frozen Charlie with a side-parted hairstyle has blue-painted eyes with white iris highlights. This pouty boy has a common Kling facial painting detail. The painted top lip curves downward on the majority of Kling dolls made from the 1880s on. Olson/Nelson Collection. (Photo: Red Kite Studios)

79. The back shoulder plate on this 3½-inch bisque shoulder head boy is marked: "300// K" inside a bell; equal length lines that form a cross; and the size number 2. The eye irises are painted the same shade of blue often used on Kling shoulder plates. The pouty turned-down mouth is a distinctive identification clue. Author's Collection. (Photo: Red Kite Studios)

80. This 6-inch bisque shoulder head has short curly red-blond hair and lobe-pierced ears. Olson/Nelson Collection. (Photo: Red Kite Studios)

81. This 4-inch unmarked bisque shoulder head with a similarly shaped shoulder plate as the shoulder head in illustration 79 has dark multi-stroke eyebrows, brown glass eyes, upper and lower eyelashes and an open/closed mouth with molded teeth. Author's Collection. (Photo: Red Kite Studios)

C.F. Kling & Co.

82. Similar to the shoulder head shown in illustration 70, this childlike 4¼-inch shoulder head has an undecorated shoulder plate. The head modeling and painting are similar to the shoulder heads in illustrations 70 and 72, although this doll has an open/closed molded mouth with a molded tongue tip. Margaret Hartshorn Collection. (Photo: Image Arts Etc.)

83. This 2¾-inch shoulder head with lobe pierced ears and upswept wavy blond hair has a finely painted scalloped design on the flared collar. An identical shoulder head doll is marked "135-6," circa 1885. Courtesy Deutsches Spielzeugmuseum, Sonneberg. (Photo: Christiane Gräfnitz)

who owned it died a few years ago, the head was still in its original wrappings as it came from Miss Robeck's great grandfather's shop, and was purchased from the woman's estate by Miss Robeck.

"This unusually lovely head has an elaborate hairdress decorated with flowers and a pink scarf, as will be seen by the pictures of the head shown following page 92. The exact date is not known, but it was one of the early heads, because the contents of the Robeck store were entirely damaged by Union soldiers during the Civil War." The caption under the photograph of the doll pictured in the St. George book is as follows: "Dresden or Parian head imported by Alma Robeck's great grandfather, an Annapolis, Maryland baker and confectioner about 1860. Found in original wrappings." Two examples of shoulder heads made from identical master molds are shown in illustrations 50 and 56.

Porcelain doll heads made by the C.F. Kling & Co. factory in the 1860s and 1870s are among the most valuable antique German dolls in collections today because they are by far the most elaborate porcelain shoulder-head dolls ever made. The hair and shoulder-plate decorations created so long ago have never been equaled by any other porcelain factory.

Chapter 4

A.W. Fr. Kister

1. The red brick building, attached to the building on the left, was the oldest building at the A.W. Fr. Kister factory site. It was torn down in 2001. (Photo: Carol Nagel)

The A.W. Fr. Kister porcelain factory, founded by Louis Oels in 1835, is located in Thuringia between the neighboring villages of Scheibe and Alsbach. The two villages, in the shadow of the Thuringian Forest, are in the upper Schwarza valley at an altitude of approximately 2000 feet. In 1996, the factory was offered for sale for one German Mark. No buyers were found, and the factory permanently closed. The three-story brick building, which contained doll-head shards from the 1840s and 1850s under the floorboards, was torn down in 2001. From studying the hundreds of Kister doll-head shards in my collection as well as shoulder heads in museums and private collections, it is my opinion that this porcelain factory made more glazed porcelain than unglazed porcelain shoulder heads.

In June of 2002, I had the privilege of interviewing a modeler who had worked for the A.W. Fr. Kister porcelain factory for more than twenty years. Her mother painted porcelain at the same factory for more than thirty years. Factory instructors taught many female employees to paint because they painted as well as their male counterparts, but worked for less money. While I was visiting the modeler's home, I noticed a beautiful porce-

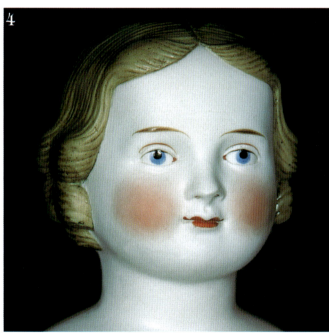

lain wreath, decorated with dozens of perfectly formed Dresden-like porcelain flowers, hanging on the wall. The molded flowers looked like those that trimmed the shoulder-head hairstyles created by Thuringian porcelain factory workers. I asked the modeler how the flowers were applied and she explained that the wreath was made in a plaster working mold, and the separate flowers were attached with porcelain slip after the wreath was removed from the mold in the leather stage and was dry enough to handle. Dresden-like flowers were also used to decorate many other types of

2. I found this doll-head shard in 1999 under the floorboards of a third-floor room during a private tour of the Kister factory. Author's Collection. (Photo: Gene Abbott)

3. A closer view of the 2½-inch glazed porcelain face shard I found in 1999 shows the typical facial-painting details found on the majority of the early glazed and unglazed shoulder heads made by this factory during the 1840s, 1850s and 1860s. The features include nearly flat eyebrows, irises without outlines or white highlights, and a very distinctive mouth. The narrow upper lip has low, far-spaced peaks and curled ends. The lower lip is rectangular in shape with rounded ends. Author's Collection. (Photo: Gene Abbott)

4. The Kister porcelain factory made this 27-inch un-tinted bisque shoulder-head doll with a modified Flat Top hairstyle featuring sharply defined curls. The painted facial features are very similar to the shard in illustration 2. The original factory body has un-tinted bisque lower arms with spoon-shaped hands. The lower legs are painted with the factory's typical garter bows. The bows match the painted bows on the bonnets seen in illustration 17. A bow of the same shape can also be seen in illustration 10, on the sixth leg from the left in the top row. Author's Collection. (Photo: Gene Abbott)

5. In 1999 storage shelves in the porcelain factory contained a small number of two-part plaster working molds. The mold of the shoulder head with a Flat Top hairstyle is concave, although it looks convex in this photograph. Author's Collection. (Photo: Gene Abbott)

6. The hairstyle on this 5½-inch Flat Top shoulder head is also similar to the comb-marked hairstyle shown in the plaster molds seen in illustration 5. The facial features include light-brown single-stroke eyebrows, gray-blue irises without an outline or a white highlight, and a painted mouth that differs slightly from the earliest dolls. The lower lip is a smaller oval shape on this shoulder head. Author's Collection. (Photo: Red Kite Studios)

7. According to a Sonneberg doll museum inventory card, this 3¾-inch Kister parian-like shoulder head was sold in 1860 by the Müller & Strassburger doll factory in Sonneberg. Note the upper and lower molded eyelids. Courtesy Deutsches Spielzeugmuseum, Sonneberg. (Photo: Christiane Gräfnitz)

8. Smaller versions of full-size shoulder heads were made by the majority of Thuringian factories that made doll-related porcelain products. These small dolls were frequently used as dollhouse dolls. This parian-like 1½-inch shoulder head has a Flat Top hairstyle similar to the image in the two-part plaster mold seen in illustration 5. Ann Meehan Collection. (Photo: Curtis Haldy)

porcelain products made by the factory from 1835 on. The A.W. Fr. Kister porcelain factory was recognized worldwide for the quality of its finished goods. The Scheibe-Alsbach factory received many awards for outstanding workmanship, including gold medals at the 1873 Vienna World Fair and the 1893 Columbian Exposition in Chicago.

The doll-related porcelain products made by this factory were unidentified until 1999, when I toured the factory and brought home 1840s and 1850s unglazed porcelain shards from under the attic floorboards. By comparing the facial painting on the china shard on page 79 with the parian-like doll in illustration 16, it becomes evident that the facial painting on factory chinas and parian-like dolls was identical from the 1850s through the 1870s.

9. This 3½-inch parian-like shoulder head with a child-like appearance has a blond center-parted hairstyle with two flat forehead curls and blue side-glancing eyes. Two vertical curls frame the face in front and rows of small curls decorate the hairstyle in back. Susan Moore Collection. (Photo: Digital Images)

10. Note the variations in size and painting detail on these nineteen Kister porcelain lower legs. A leg with the same painted ribbon design as the bonnet ties on the pair of dolls shown in illustration 17 is pictured on the top row. Author's Collection. (Photo: Gene Abbott)

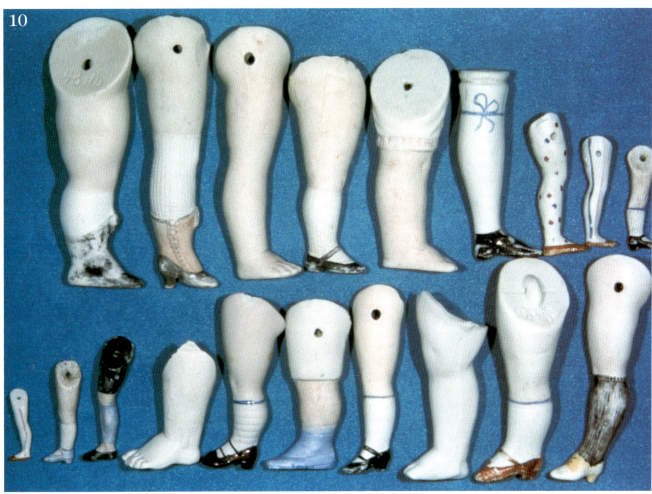

11. This glazed-porcelain 5½-inch shoulder head is typical of the variety of chinas made at the factory during the 1860s and 1870s. The elaborate black hairstyle contains a long vertical curl on each side of the face. Note the typical 1860s factory painted features. Kenneth Drew Collection. (Photo: Ann Hanat)

12. The A.W. Fr. Kister porcelain factory made a large variety of chinas and parian-like shoulder heads with 1860s and 1870s fancy hairstyles. This 2-inch doll-head shard has earring holes pierced into the head. The blond comb-marked pageboy hairstyle has a large braid that encircles the head. The back hairstyle features a molded ribbon tied in a bow. A ribbon divides the smooth upper-crown section from the two rows of vertical curls molded on the lower half of the head. Author's Collection. (Photo: Red Kite Studios)

13. A focal point of the back hairstyle on the shoulder head seen in illustration 11 is a gold-trimmed black snood that covers the smoothly combed hair on top and the chignon below. A wide black headband is molded across the hair. Kenneth Drew Collection. (Photo: Ann Hanat)

14. This 1½-inch Kister head shard contains an unusual molded hairstyle. The long blond wavy hair in front features braids that encircle each ear. The black lattice-like snood is bordered by a molded blue ruffle on top of the head and two matching ruffles on the nape of the neck. Author's Collection. (Photo: Red Kite Studios)

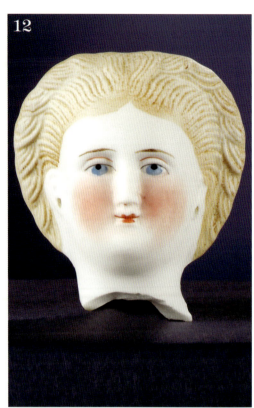

15. The back hairstyle of the doll in illustration 16 has hair puffs, a diagonal roll of hair and a half-circle braid on the nape of the neck. The back shoulder plate is marked with a size number. Private Collection. (Photo: Anne Friis)

16. This fine example of a Kister parian-like doll with a fancy hairstyle has facial painting similar to that of a black-haired china shoulder-head shard I found at the factory in 1999. The front hairstyle has a molded braid holding three large hair puffs in place. Two small flat curls are molded on the forehead. Note the upper and lower eyelid sculpting. The neck is partially covered by an auction tag. The facial painting is also similar to the 27-inch doll in illustration 4. Private Collection. (Photo: Anne Friis)

Two parian-like dolls wear molded yellow bonnets with rose ribbons tied under the chins and multi-colored flowers attached to the brim facings. The bows painted under the chins are typical of the A.W. Fr. Kister porcelain factory. They are painted with same bow configuration as the garter ties decorating many of the factory's bisque lower legs. Margaret Hartshorn Collection. (Photo: Margaret Hartshorn)

CHAPTER 4

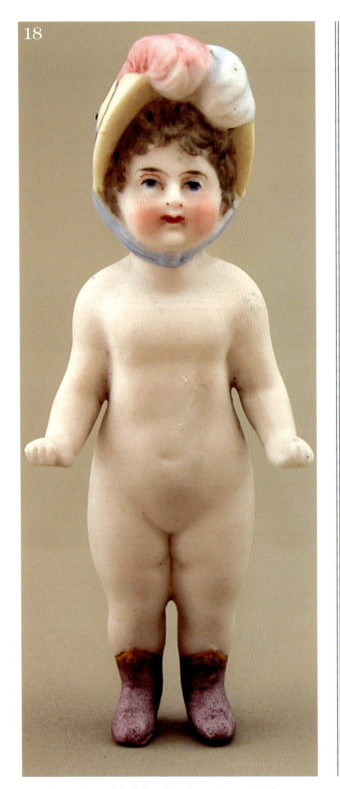
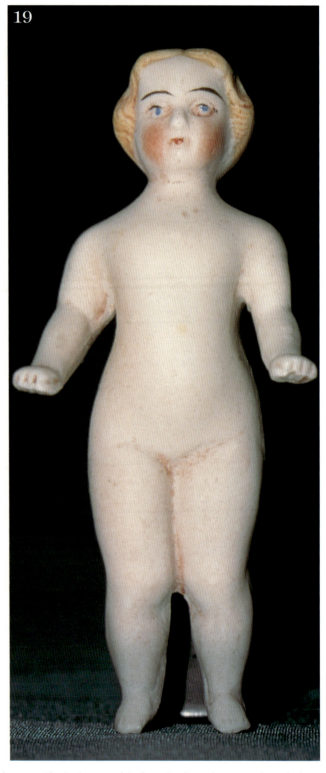

18. Unjointed porcelain dolls referred to as Frozen Charlottes were made by many Thuringian porcelain factories from the 1850s through the 1930s. This 3¾-inch parian-like shoulder head has short curly gray-brown hair and a pale-yellow bonnet trimmed with two molded feathers. A blue ribbon is tied under the chin. Although the doll is very small, the typical factory mouth painting is evident. This doll belonged to a former modeler of the porcelain factory. Author's Collection. (Photo: Gene Abbott)

19. This 2½-inch Frozen Charlotte shard has a chubby body and bent arms with clenched hands and palms facing down. Author's Collection. (Photo: Gene Abbott)

20. Another example of a Kister bisque dollhouse doll, this 2¼-inch doll has different head modeling than those shown in illustrations 21 and 22. The original military uniforms differ only in the placement of the attached medals. Realistic age wrinkles are special features on all three of the Kister dollhouse dolls seen in this chapter. Ann Meehan Collection. (Photo: Curtis Haldy)

21. This 2-inch bisque shoulder head has brown painted hair, single-stroke eyebrows, a molded mustache and a long beard. Ann Meehan Collection. (Photo: Curtis Haldy)

22. The Kister factory made many doll-related porcelain products, including dollhouse dolls. (The Ciesliks' book, *German Doll Studies*, includes two photographs of dollhouse dolls made by the factory). This bisque example has a 1¾-inch shoulder head with blue painted eyes, gray multi-stroke eyebrows, a mustache and "mutton chops" facial hair. Ann Meehan Collection. (Photo: Curtis Haldy)

Chapter 5

Conta & Böhme

Porcelain shoulder heads made by the Conta & Böhme porcelain factory in Pössneck were unidentified until 2001. Doll collectors worldwide can now identify many Conta & Böhme dolls in their collections because of a 2001 self-published book, titled *Conta & Boehme Porcelain, Identification and Value Guide,* by Janice and Richard Vogel. The Vogels have collected Conta & Böhme porcelain products for more than thirty years. Their important 296-page book, a collaborative effort between Pössneck historian Hans Walter Enkelmann and the Vogels, documents the history of the factory as well as the wide variety of products made for 117 years.

It is well worth visiting the town museum in Pössneck to study the outstanding collection of porcelain products made by the Conta & Böhme porcelain factory. Hans Enkelmann lists many products made by the factory in his well-researched booklet, *Jahre Goethe in Pössneck,* on Pössneck. The list includes: "candelabras, jardinières, figurines of holy people, containers for holy water, animals, tobacco boxes, ashtray stands, match holders, menu holders, writing utensils, jewelry and mirror boxes, vases, sconces, bathing children, toy dolls and wall reliefs." A small glass case in the museum is of considerable interest to antique doll collectors. It contains many Conta & Böhme doll-head shards and Frozen Charlotte shards. One larger doll-head shard is very distinctive. Two versions of this shoulder head, made from an iden-

tical master mold, are pictured in illustrations 29 and 33. The doll-head shards in the Pössneck museum, pictured in the Vogel book, provide visual confirmation of porcelain shoulder heads made by this factory. Heretofore, these doll heads were listed as "maker unknown."

The Vogels cover the history of the Conta & Böhme porcelain factory from its founding in 1800 until its closing in 1931. The discovery of the factory's porcelain shards is described in detail in their book. The shards were found in 1981 during the demolition of a two-story house located at 24 Saalfelder Street in Pössneck. Conta & Böhme porcelain articles were used as part of the fill between the first and second floor of this historically important 1814 building. The 1814 city plan found in the Pössneck archives shows that the Conta & Böhme porcelain factory was once located in this building.

The doll-head shards of interest to doll collectors are pictured beginning on page 75 of the Vogel book. Forty-seven shards are pictured in black-and-white photographs showing front, side and back views of each doll. The distinctive hairstyles and facial sculpting are accurately captured in each photograph.

Even the founding date of the Conta & Böhme porcelain factory was in question until Hans Enkelmann discovered an original letter in the town archives dated December 6, 1800, granting Tobias C. Albert permission to found the Pössneck porcelain factory. The incorrect date of 1790 is listed in many porcelain books. In February 2004, I wrote to Hans Enkelmann asking if he could date the initial production of porce-

1. This is the oldest factory building still standing on the factory site. A former clock tower is visible on the left corner of the 1865 building. A semi-circle addition is evident on the right side of the building, which originally contained the office of the production chief. (Photo: Hans Enkelmann)

2. An enlarged copy of a Conta & Böhme letterhead illustration shows the buildings that were on the factory site around 1900. Only three of these buildings are still standing today. The building shown in illustration 1 is located below and to the right of the smokestack on the original factory letterhead. Courtesy Hans Enkelmann.

CHAPTER 5

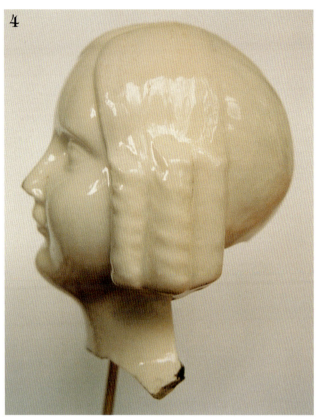

3. In June 2004, Hans Enkelmann photographed this early glazed-porcelain 3¾-inch head shard found on the factory grounds. Fingerprints inside the head indicate the porcelain mixture was pressed into the mold. Courtesy Pössneck Town Museum. (Photo: Hans Enkelmann)

4. Talented factory sculptors created this unusual center-parted hairstyle featuring three vertical curls and a smooth back head devoid of modeling details. The KPM Berlin porcelain factory made a similar head with four vertical curls in 1845. Courtesy Pössneck Town Museum. (Photo: Hans Enkelmann)

88

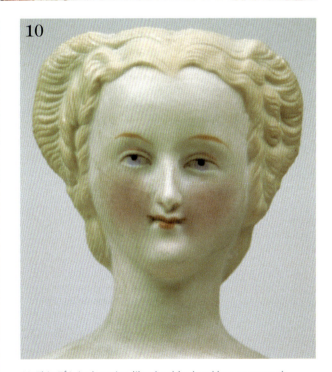

5. This 2-inch parian-like shoulder-head shard was also found on the porcelain factory grounds. The blond molded hair is flared around the face from a center part. Courtesy Pössneck Town Museum. (Photo: Hans Enkelmann)

6. The side view of the shoulder head in illustration 5 shows the "ridge" of flared comb-marked hair that encircles the head. Courtesy Pössneck Town Museum. (Photo: Hans Enkelmann)

7. The back hairstyle of the shoulder head seen in illustration 5 is unusual. The hair on each side of the back part line is combed to the sides of the head, exposing a section of long comb-marked hair in the center. The Conta & Böhme porcelain factory made several variations of this hairstyle. Two variations of similar back hairstyles are pictured in illustrations 9 and 37. Courtesy Pössneck Town Museum. (Photo: Hans Enkelmann)

8. This 4½-inch parian-like shoulder head has similar facial modeling as the doll head shard in illustration 5. The sculpted upper eyelids create a heavy-lidded "sleepy" look. The hairstyle is decorated with an applied molded rose, green leaves and gold beads. A doll-head shard pictured in illustration 159 on page 90 of *Conta & Boehme Porcelain, Identification and Value Guide* by Janice and Richard Vogel has a similar hairstyle. Margaret Hartshorn Collection. (Photo: Margaret Hartshorn)

9. The back view of the hairstyle seen in illustration 8 shows the twisted knot of hair on the nape of the neck and the strand of molded gold beads decorating the hair. Margaret Hartshorn Collection. (Photo: Margaret Hartshorn)

10. This 5½-inch parian-like shoulder head has an unusual triangular-shaped hairstyle featuring braids on each side of the face, a center part and comb-marked hair. Its facial modeling is similar to that of the factory shard and shoulder head pictured in illustrations 5 and 8. Courtesy Deutsches Spielzeugmueum, Sonneberg. (Photo: Christiane Gräfnitz)

Chapter 5

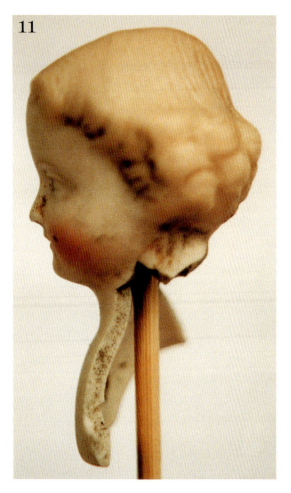

11. Another doll-head shard photographed in June 2004 by Hans Enkelmann provides proof that the factory made simple Flat Top hairstyles in the 1860s as well as fancy hairstyles. Courtesy Pössneck Town Museum. (Photo: Hans Enkelmann)

12. The Conta & Böhme porcelain factory made a variety of parian-like shoulder heads with simple hairstyles, including this 4½-inch blond-haired shoulder head with a swivel neck and modified Flat Top hairstyle. Olson/Nelson Collection. (Photo: Red Kite Studios)

13. This 5-inch parian-like shoulder head has a round face, light-blond wavy hair, large blue glass eyes, typical sculpted eyelids and a painted mouth. A painted-eye version of this shoulder head (not shown) has the typical factory eyes with half-pupils and irises. Large flat curls encircle the back of the head. Olson/Nelson Collection. (Photo: Red Kite Studios)

14. This 2-inch parian-like shoulder head with a short curly hairstyle and a dark-blue ribbon headband is marked with the size number "6." This head is similar to a head shard pictured in illustration 143 on page 86 in the Vogels' book. Susan Moore Collection. (Photo: Digital Images)

lain doll heads. He kindly answered, providing the following information: "It is assumed that doll heads were made in Pössneck as early as 1845. The head from Janice Vogel's book page 77 (top) may date back to this time. Although Ms. Vogel has depicted 47 different doll heads the number of heads is probably twice or three times as high. The heads in these pictures (I sent the whole lot to her in America so that she could take photos of them) were found by chance.

"They are all rejects, that is, pieces which were thrown away because they were faulty. I found some of them when I was excavating on the factory premises. Others were found when old houses in Pössneck were pulled down. This can be explained: a lot of porcelain painters worked for Conta & Böhme. Many of them lived next to the premises. Others, the so-called home painters, worked from home. Each week they picked up baskets full of doll heads from the factory, painted them at home and took them back to the factory to the kilns. Sometimes, when a piece would not turn out nicely or had some kind of fault, it was dumped somewhere on the private grounds of the house, in a loft or shed. There was no trash collection."

Not only does excavation uncover porcelain shards that identify the products made by a particular porcelain factory, but remod-

eling of old buildings can also provide important clues to the past. In their book, the Vogels picture and describe a very important porcelain disc that was discovered in 1995 in the ball of an old Pössneck church spire. The porcelain disc contains the names of Conta & Böhme porcelain factory employees and their respective titles. It lists the names and job titles of thirty porcelain factory employees. The number of employees for each category and their respective titles are: one manager of the technical division, one trainee who is also a color laboratory technician, one accountant, thirteen artists, one apprentice (no type of work listed), one first burner who is also a capsule lathe operator, one *Masse* miller, together with three (unnamed) burners, four (unnamed) day laborers, five lathe operators and two apprentice lathe operators. This list of jobs is similar to the division of labor in the majority of large Thuringian porcelain factories.

It is fortunate for doll collectors that Janice Vogel decided to write a book on Conta & Böhme porcelain products. It is also fortunate that Pössneck historian Hans Enkelmann sent Janice a large box of doll-head shards that he found on the Conta & Böhme factory grounds for her to photograph and return. Because she included forty-seven doll-head shards in her book, we can now identify these beautifully sculpted and painted glazed and unglazed shoulder head dolls.

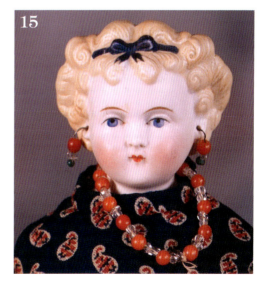

15. This example has a head and hairstyle modeling similar to that of the shoulder head pictured in illustration 14. The painted ribbon headband is tied in a bow on this example. This 3½-inch shoulder head has molded eyelids, pierced ears and well-defined curls covering the back of the head. Terry Schmeltzer Collection. (Photo: Estelle Johnston)

CHAPTER 5

16. This 3-inch shoulder head has lobe-pierced ears and finely painted brush strokes at the temples. The black molded hair is styled with three rows of waves in front of three rows of vertical curls on each side of a center part. Three separate ribbons decorate the back of the head. One of the ribbons holds the cluster of curls arranged on the nape of the neck. The doll head shard pictured in illustration 123 on page 80 in the Vogels' book was made from an identical master mold. Susan Moore Collection. (Photo: Digital Images)

17. This 3-inch shoulder head has pierced ears, well-defined waves on either side of a center part and a molded headband. The back hairstyle contains a large braided bun. Olson/Nelson Collection. (Photo: Red Kite Studios)

18. This 7½-inch parian-like dollhouse doll with a 2-inch shoulder head was made from a master mold identical to the one used to make the doll in Illustration 16. Ann Meehan Collection. (Photo: Curtis Haldy)

19. A close view of a 4-inch parian-like bald shoulder head shows facial painting typical of the factory, especially the mouth painting with high upper-lip peaks and curled ends. The blue painted eyes have a white highlight on the right side of each iris. The factory painted iris highlights on both the left and right sides of the irises. Author's Collection. (Photo: Gregg Smith)

20. The parian-like shoulder head shown in illustration 19 has pierced ears and wears an original mohair wig. Author's Collection. (Photo: Red Kite Studios)

21. The shoulder head shown in illustrations 19 and 20 has a netlike covering, referred to as a snood, to hold the hair on the mohair wig in place. Author's Collection. (Red Kite Studios)

Chapter 5

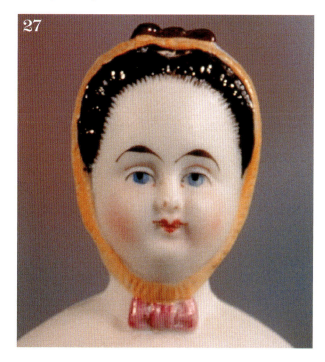

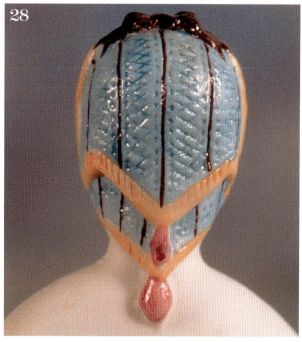

27. This 2¾-inch brown-haired parian-like shoulder head with similar brush marks around the hairline as the doll in illustration 24 wears a colorful folded scarf on her head. A molded bow decorates the center of this unusual headdress. A second bow is tied under the chin. Terry Schmeltzer Collection. (Photo: Estelle Johnston)

28. A back view of the doll in illustration 27 shows the aqua scarf with maroon stripes and wide yellow edging. A pink tassel is molded on the shoulders. Terry Schmeltzer Collection. (Photo: Estelle Johnston)

22. An unpainted bead necklace is a focal point on this 4½-inch parian-like shoulder head. Its center-parted hairstyle is similar to the hairstyle on a shoulder head made by the C.F. Kling & Co. porcelain factory and shown in illustration 50. The facial painting, especially that of the mouth, varies from the painting on Kling shoulder heads. A similar hairstyle is pictured in illustration 158 on page 90 in the Vogels' book. The front hairstyles are identical, although the back styling varies slightly. Olson/Nelson Collection. (Photo: Red Kite Studios)

23. The long hairstyle of the shoulder head in illustration 22 is decorated with a molded comb trimmed with large white beads. The Vogels' book shows a number of dolls with long hair wearing similarly trimmed combs. Olson/Nelson Collection. (Photo: Red Kite Studios)

24. This 2¼-inch brown-haired parian-like doll with comb marks has a similar brush-stroked hairline as the one in illustration 26. Facial features are identical on many glazed- and unglazed-porcelain shoulder heads made by this factory. Susan Moore Collection. (Photo: Digital Images)

25. The back view of the doll in illustration 24 shows the hair roll encircling the head, a smooth center section and large black bow made of hair. A shoulder head made from the same master mold, with a red molded bow, is in the collection of The Shelburne Museum in Vermont. Susan Moore Collection. (Photo: Digital Images)

26. This 3½-inch glazed-porcelain shoulder head with uncommon comb-marked brown hair has long braids encircling the head and fine brushstrokes painted around the hairline. The "sleepy" painted eyes with molded upper eyelids are typical facial features of the Conta & Böhme porcelain factory. The shoulder plate includes a slightly molded bust and deeply sloping shoulders. A molded snood decorates the back hairstyle. Susan Moore Collection. (Photo: Frank McAloon)

Chapter 5

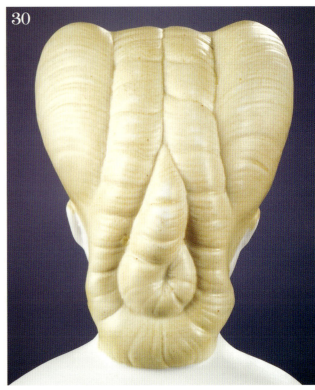

29. This 4¾-inch parian-like shoulder head was made from a master mold identical to the one used to make the glazed-porcelain shoulder head in illustration 33. The ribbed comb is painted the same color as the hair and it matches the comb on the black-haired china. A similar hairstyle is pictured in illustration 149 on page 87 in the Vogels' book. Olson/Nelson Collection. (Photo: Red Kite Studios)

30. The back view of the shoulder head in illustration 29 shows the long rolls of twisted looped hair. Olson/Nelson Collection. (Photo: Red Kite Studios)

31. The hair on this 4-inch shoulder head is combed back from the face into well-defined flat curls. The curls are held by a headband painted the same color as the hair. The back hairstyle features loosely curled hair. Other facial features include large "sleepy" eyes and an unpainted space between the upper and lower lips. Kenneth Drew Collection. (Photo: Ann Hanat)

32. A small glass case in the Pössneck Town Museum contains a number of Conta & Böhme shoulder head shards found on the porcelain factory grounds. A group of these heads form a line. One shard is taller than the rest. Examples of this shoulder head are shown in illustrations 29, 30 and 33. (Photo: Mary Krombholz)

33 The factory used identical plaster working molds in various sizes to make glazed and unglazed shoulder heads. This glazed-porcelain 4½-inch shoulder head has pierced ears, a wide ribbed comb, and hair puffs arranged on each side of a center part. The shoulder head is similar to the taller shoulder head shard in the glass case pictured in illustration 32. Olson/Nelson Collection. (Photo: Red Kite Studios)

34. The hairstyle of a head shard in the Vogels' book shows a strand of molded beads decorating the hairstyle. The Conta & Böhme porcelain factory made several variations of hairstyles featuring molded beads. In the example shown in illustrations 36 and 37, the beads are painted the same color as the hair while on this example, gold-painted beads trim the flared hair behind the braids. Margaret Hartshorn Collection. (Photo: Image Arts Etc.)

35. The side view of the hair on the shard in illustration 34 shows the two separate strands of gold beads above and below each ear. Margaret Hartshorn Collection. (Photo: Image Arts Etc.)

36. Another example has larger braids in front and a more defined center-part line than the shard in illustration 34. Terry Schmeltzer Collection. (Photo: Estelle Johnston)

37. The back hair of the example in illustration 36 is styled in a similar manner as the that of the doll-head shard in illustration 7. The waved hair is combed to each side of the head in a V-shaped pattern, leaving a center section. This example has a large braided bun between the sections of hair. The two strands of beads are evident on each side of the head. Terry Schmeltzer Collection. (Photo: Estelle Johnston)

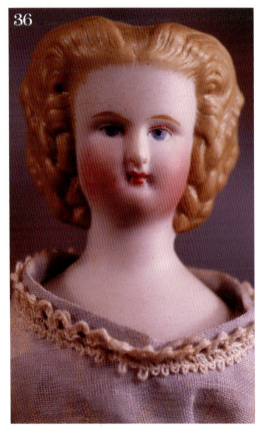

CONTA & BÖHME

38. This 4¾-inch parian-like shoulder head has an unusual hairstyle featuring a molded rose and leaves under the exposed ears. The hairstyle also includes a large braid that encircles the head. Many small flat curls are molded on each side of the center part. Margaret Hartshorn Collection. (Photo: Image Arts Etc.)

39. The back view of the shoulder head in illustration 38 shows the blue comb holding the unusual large braided bun. Rows of horizontal curls are molded on each side of the head. Margaret Hartshorn Collection. (Photo: Image Arts Etc.)

40. Yet another example has more visible strands of beads in front due to the lack of molded braids in front. The back hairstyle features braids and a molded bun. Margaret Hartshorn Collection. (Photo: Image Arts Etc.)

41. This 7-inch parian-like doll has a 1¾-inch shoulder head. The smoothly combed hairstyle features a molded snood in back. The headband is painted the same color as the hair. A doll-head shard pictured in illustration 138 on page 84 in the Vogels' book matches this head. Susan Moore Collection. (Photo: Digital Images)

Chapter 5

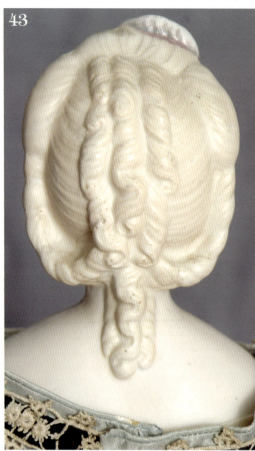

42. Two molded feathers inserted into a round holder decorate the front of the pale-blond hairstyle on this 4¼-inch shoulder head. A large braid is molded on each side of the face, leaving the lobes of the pierced ears exposed. Margaret Hartshorn Collection. (Photo: Image Arts Etc.)

43. The back hairstyle features three long vertical curls that spill onto the shoulder plate. Margaret Hartshorn Collection. (Photo: Image Arts Etc.)

44. This 4½-inch shoulder head has tan flared hair styled with a deeply molded center part. Painted blue eyes have the typical factory "sleepy" look because the half-pupils and irises are painted as if they continue under the upper eyelids. Margaret Hartshorn Collection. (Photo: Margaret Hartshorn)

45. The back view of the shoulder head in illustration 44 shows the unusual arrangement of hair that surrounds the large elaborate braided bun. Margaret Hartshorn Collection. (Photo: Margaret Hartshorn)

46. This parian-like shoulder head was made from a master mold identical to the one used to make the china example in illustration 46. The head features include blue painted eyes, tan one-stroke eyebrows and "sleepy" eyes. Margaret Hartshorn Collection. (Photo: Image Arts Etc.)

47. The side view shows another special highlight of the shoulder head seen in illustration 46: a daisy-like flower with streamers decorates each side of the snood. Margaret Hartshorn Collection. (Photo: Image Arts Etc.)

48. This uncommon 3¼-inch glazed porcelain shoulder head has many special attributes. The hair is shaded from light blond in front to brown in back. A blue porcelain ruffle holds the molded snood in place. Margaret Hartshorn Collection. (Photo: Image Arts Etc.)

CHAPTER 5

49. This 3¾-inch shoulder head has a distinctive black hairstyle with flared hair around the face. The back hairstyle includes a smooth comb-marked crown with twisted hair arranged on the nape of the neck. Margaret Hartshorn Collection. (Photo: Image Arts Etc.)

50. This 5½-inch shoulder head has an elaborate black hairstyle featuring crown-like puffs that form a triangle on top of the head. A shoulder-head shard pictured in illustration 136 on page 84 in the Vogels' book was made from an identical master mold. Kenneth Drew Collection. (Photo: Ann Hanat)

51. The back of the head seen in illustration 50 shows the molded comb between the smooth center section and the snood-covered chignon. Kenneth Drew Collection. (Photo: Ann Hanat)

CONTA & BÖHME

52. This parian-like doll-head shard was found on the Conta & Böhme porcelain factory grounds. The long hairstyle features 1870s height above the crown. The shoulder heads pictured in illustrations 54 and 55 were made from identical master molds as this doll-head shard. Courtesy Pössneck Town Museum. (Photo: Hans Enkelmann)

53. Rows of long vertical curls cover the entire back of the head shown in illustration 52. Courtesy Pössneck Town Museum. (Photo: Hans Enckelmann)

54. The headband is painted gold on this black-haired shoulder head made from a master mold similar to the one used to make the doll-head shard in illustration 52. The blue-painted irises have large white highlights on the right side of each iris. The blue ribbon necklace, tied in a bow on the back of the neck, holds an unusual large molded unpainted ring. Courtesy Olga's Fancy Museum in Copenhagen, Denmark. (Photo: Anne Friis)

55. This 4-inch shoulder head was made from a similar master mold as the doll-head shard shown in illustration 52. The typical factory facial features include eye pupils painted close to the top lid, rather than centered. The long blond wavy hair, with 1870s height above the crown, is held in place by a gold comb. The temples are painted with fine brush marks. Courtesy Deutches Spielzeugmuseum, Sonneberg. (Photo: Christiane Gräfnitz)

Chapter 5

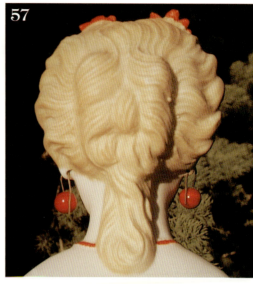

56. This rare Conta & Böhme 4¾-inch shoulder head has a flower-trimmed comb on the crown of the head. Each comb mark is evident on this well-sculpted short blond hairstyle. Pierced ears, realistic upper and lower eyelids and typical factory eye and mouth painting are focal points of this doll. Another special feature is the large red molded cross hanging from a red bead necklace encircling the neck. A similar hairstyle is pictured in illustration 139 on page 85 of the Vogels' book. Barbara Kouri Collection. (Photo: John Kouri)

57. The back of the head shows the comb-marked hair styled with waves and hair rolls that end on the shoulders. The back shoulder plate is marked with the number "16." Barbara Kouri Collection. (Photo: John Kouri)

58. This 1½-inch parian-like shoulder head has an upswept hairstyle trimmed with an unusual molded comb. Ann Meehan Collection. (Photo: Curtis Haldy)

59. This 6-inch dollhouse doll was made from a master mold identical to the one used for the examples in illustrations 60 and 61. It is evident that factory artists gave the same attention to detail on large and small dolls. Author's Collection. (Photo: Gregg Smith)

60. This view of another example of the doll in illustration 61 shows the molded upper eyelids, "sleepy" eyes and comb-marked hair. The mouth includes the typical factory widely spaced high upper-lip peaks and curls at each end. This example has very large earring holes. Courtesy Olga's Fancy Museum in Copenhagen, Denmark. (Photo: Anne Friis)

61. An elaborate blond hairstyle and blue glass eyes are special features on this 4½-inch shoulder head. The curly 1870s-type hairstyle has bangs and long curls arranged behind and in front of the pierced ears. Margaret Hartshorn Collection. (Photo: Image Arts Etc.)

62. The back view of the hairstyle shown in illustration 61 is equally elaborate. It has multiple rolls of hair arranged on each side of the back center part. A small braid and hair loops are also featured on this comb-marked hairstyle. Margaret Hartshorn Collection. (Photo: Image Arts Etc.)

Chapter 6

Simon & Halbig

In 1869, the Simon & Halbig porcelain factory was founded by Carl Halbig and Wilhelm Simon in Gräfenhain, Thuringia. An article by Adrian Weber in the April 17, 1999, issue of the newspaper *Kreis Gotha* provides an interesting history of Carl Halbig. The title of the article is: "Porcelain Dolls in Silk Dresses: The Mansion of Manufacturer Carl Halbig of Gräfenhain. A portion of the article reads: "For about a hundred years, a mansion on a hillside has ruled the silhouette of the village Gräfenhain on the north side of the Thüringer Wald (Thuringian Forest). The residents call this stately building 'the villa,' and only a few know about the eventful history of the house with the address 'Am Berg 2' today. Until his death in 1926, here lived 'Secret' Commerce Council Carl Halbig, a local porcelain manufacturer and 'charity person' of the town.

"Carl Halbig was born on January 13, 1839. He was trained to be an accountant, and then started his job with the Alt, Beck & Gottschalck Company in the neighboring village of Nauendorf. The company manufactured porcelain dolls and all types of tableware. The business went very well at that time, and so at age 29 Halbig decided to go out on his own. With the help of Mr. Simon from Hildburghausen, he bought the old pastor house on Hauptstrasse (Main Street)

1. The Simon & Halbig porcelain factory in Gräfenhain was torn down in the mid-1990s. (Photo: Carol Nagel)

2. This beautifully modeled and painted parian-like doll has a 4-inch shoulder head with a center-parted hairstyle, black gold-edged headband, light-brown multi-stroke eyebrows, upper and lower eyelashes, large molded earrings and a black ribbon necklace with a gold cross pendant. The blue painted eyes are unusual because of the wide shaded gray line below the finer black line that outlines the upper eyelids. This feature, found on the earliest dolls, creates a soft dreamy look. Estelle Johnston Collection. (Photo: Estelle Johnston)

3. This 2½-inch shoulder head was made from a master mold identical to that used to make the shoulder head in illustration 2. It has an applied rose and leaves on the molded headband, multi-stroke eyebrows and finely painted upper and lower eyelashes. Unusual shadows accentuate the realistic painted eyes. A common painted feature that identifies Simon & Halbig parian-like dolls is the heavy black outlining of the upper eyelids. Margaret Hartshorn Collection. (Photo: Margaret Hartshorn)

4. The hair on this 4-inch parian-like shoulder head is pulled smoothly back into a circle of curls on the back of the head. The Sonneberg museum's inventory card indicates it was made in 1875 and donated by Simon & Halbig in 1910. Courtesy Deutsches Spielzeugmuseum, Sonneberg. (Photo: Christiane Gräfnitz)

5. The back view of the shoulder head in illustration 4 shows the small circle of braids on the crown of the head and the long comb-marked hair with a cluster of curls molded on the shoulders. Courtesy Deutsches Spielzeugmuseum, Sonneberg. (Photo: Christiane Gräfnitz)

CHAPTER 6

6. This early lady doll has a 6-inch shoulder head marked "S10H." A large black molded bow decorates the top of the head. Facial features include heavily outlined upper eyelids, fully outlined irises, and an M-shaped upper-lip accent line. According to the Sonneberg museum's inventory card, the 1875 shoulder head was donated to the museum in 1910 by the Simon & Halbig porcelain factory. It is pictured in color plate 115 on page 250 in the Ciesliks' *German Doll Encyclopedia*. Courtesy Deutsches Spielzeugmuseum, Sonneberg. (Photo: Christiane Gräfnitz)

7. This 3-inch shoulder head has a swivel neck, glass eyes, pierced ears and a black molded bow. The identical shoulder heads shown in illustrations 8, 9 and 10 exemplify the exquisite appeal of early Simon & Halbig shoulder-head dolls with molded hair. Terry Schmeltzer Collection. (Photo: Estelle Johnston)

8. This 3¼-inch glass-eyed shoulder head with a swivel neck has a flat green bow decorating the upswept wavy hairstyle. The head features include blue glass eyes, multi-stroke eyebrows and upper and lower eyelashes. Margaret Hartshorn Collection. (Photo: Margaret Hartshorn)

9. Two large comb-marked braids cover the back of the head of the shoulder head seen in illustration 8. Margaret Hartshorn Collection. (Photo: Margaret Hartshorn)

10

This 4-inch shoulder head with a swivel neck has an upswept hairdo trimmed with a flat green bow. It was made from a master mold identical to the one used to make the shoulder head in illustration 8. Head features include a swivel neck, pierced-in ears (with the earring hole pierced directly into the head instead of the earlobe), light-brown multi-stroke eyebrows and upper and lower eyelashes. The light-red lips are finely outlined in coral. A double braid covers the back of the head. Estelle Johnston Collection. (Photo: Estelle Johnston)

11. This 15-inch shoulder-head doll has a deeply sculpted center part dividing the upswept wavy hairstyle. The unusual painted eyes have outlined irises with a semi-circle of tiny white highlights painted below the pupils. The upper eyelids are heavily outlined in black. The back hairstyle features large braids across the crown and loosely curled hair below. Estelle Johnston Collection. (Photo: Estelle Johnston)

12. This 4¾-inch shoulder-head doll is wearing an original dress made of tan cotton, trimmed with red silk ribbons and lace. Multi-stroke eyebrows and upper and lower eyelashes frame the threaded blue glass eyes. The short curly hair is trimmed with a ribbon and an off-center bow. Margaret Hartshorn Collection. (Photo: Margaret Hartshorn)

13. This 4-inch parian-like shoulder head with a swivel neck has large blue glass eyes accented with multi-stroke eyebrows, upper and lower eyelashes and typical factory facial painting. The upswept hairdo includes well-defined waves and curls encircled by a blue molded ribbon. Margaret Hartshorn Collection. (Photo: Image Arts Etc.)

14. Two uncommon dolls with 4-inch shoulder heads have similar center-parted hairstyles. The doll on the left has a headband painted the same color as the hair, while the other has a rose-painted headband. Both have multi-stroke eyebrows and upper and lower eyelashes. Estelle Johnston Collection. (Photo: Estelle Johnston)

15. The back view of two identical heads shows the deeply molded indentations between the sections of hair. One doll has a separate shoulder plate with a swivel neck while the other has a one-piece shoulder head with a blue ribbon necklace and bow. Estelle Johnston Collection. (Photo: Estelle Johnston)

Chapter 6

16. This 8-inch all-bisque doll with an Alice in Wonderland hairstyle has light brown single-stroke eyebrows, a simple blond hairstyle and pink luster boots. The heavy black outlines of the upper eyelids are evident in this photograph. Susan Moore Collection. (Photo: Digital Images)

17. The Simon & Halbig porcelain factory made this 2½-inch shoulder head with short curly reddish-blond hair. The right eye has a thicker black line outlining the upper eyelid than the left eye. Susan Moore Collection. (Photo: Digital Images)

18. This 4¼-inch shoulder head has brown upswept hair and a black molded headband. The front shoulder plate is marked "S5H." Olson/Nelson Collection. (Photo: Red Kite Studios)

19. This shoulder head is also shown in color plate 118 on page 77 of the Cieslik's *German Doll Encyclopedia*. The color section of this encyclopedia pictures a group of Simon & Halbig parian-like shoulder heads marked with SH initials and a size number. The head features include a curly blond hairstyle with a black headband, single-stroke eyebrows and fully outlined blue irises. Susan Moore Collection. (Photo: Digital Images)

20

This doll with a lightly tinted 4-inch shoulder head has a short, curly comb-marked hairstyle. The facial features include multi-stroke eyebrows, threaded-blue glass eyes, upper and lower painted eyelashes and an M-shaped darker lip-accent line between the upper and lower lips. Another typical factory identification feature are the underarm definition lines that form a V. The marked boy in illustration 50 has these identical lines. Author's Collection. (Photo: Lee Krombholz)

Chapter 6

21. This 4-inch shoulder head has painted blue eyes and thick black upper eyelid lines. The typical factory lip-accent line follows the curve of the upper lip to form the letter "M." The Simon & Halbig porcelain factory was founded in 1869. The factory introduced parian-like dolls with simple Flat Top and modified Flat Top hairstyles during doll production in the 1870s. Other Thuringian porcelain factories made shoulder heads with Flat Top hairstyles in the early 1860s, before making "fancies" later in the same decade. Susan Moore Collection. (Photo: Digital Images)

22. This 2-inch shoulder head with a wide Flat Top hairstyle has typical factory facial painting that includes generously blushed cheeks. Olson/Nelson Collection. (Photo: Red Kite Studios)

in Gräfenhain in March of 1868, and had it furnished as a porcelain factory. After one year of work, porcelain production began in 1869.

"In the beginning, dolls dressed in delicate silk outfits were made of 'biscuit' porcelain. Later the company specialized in doll heads made in many different styles. The girl toys (with the cardboard box mark sitting chinaman) were loved mainly in Great Britain and America. That must be the reason that most of the products of the porcelain factory in Gräfenhain are nowadays found in North America. After his partner's death in 1894, the company became the sole property of Halbig, who became the largest employer in town.

"The flourishing business made it possible for him to become very generous in his hometown. His charity efforts earned him the respect of the residents, and in 1893 he was awarded the title of 'Commerce Council.' Towards the end of the year 1900, the Halbigs were able to move into the 'villa' on the hillside, which would turn into a retirement home for the 61-year-old industrialist. The four-floor building has a wonderful view of Ohrdruf and Gotha.

"With the beginning of World War I, the lucrative exporting business collapsed. During the inflation years after the war, the doll production would never reach the

23. This 6-inch shoulder head illustrates the trademark factory painting of eyebrows, eyes and mouths on parian-like dolls made from the 1870s on. Note the large fully outlined blue irises and darker M-shaped line between the upper and lower lips. Olson/Nelson Collection. (Photo: Red Kite Studios)

24. This 4½-inch shoulder head is similar to the one shown in illustration 23. It has pierced ears and generously blushed cheeks. Olson/Nelson Collection. (Photo: Red Kite Studios)

25. This 5¼-inch glass-eyed shoulder head with short curly hair and pierced ears has multi-stroke eyebrows, upper and lower lashes and an M-shaped lip accent line. Olson/Nelson Collection. (Photo: Red Kite Studios)

Chapter 6

26. This 3¾-inch all-bisque doll, made from a master mold similar to the one used to makes the doll in illustration 16, has unusual painted shoes and socks. The pink luster boots are identical to those worn by the larger doll, except that the painted socks are banded by a scalloped pink luster border. Susan Moore Collection. (Photo: Digital Images)

27. These redressed Simon & Halbig all-bisque dolls have painted socks and shoes identical to those on several other Simon & Halbig all-bisque dolls pictured in this chapter. The 5-inch-high doll has a Flat Top hairstyle and the 4-inch-high doll has an Alice in Wonderland hairstyle. Author's Collection. (Photo: Lee Krombholz)

pre-war position again. A further big blow for Halbig was the sudden death of his son Arno in 1923. Three years later, on June 23rd at the age of 86, Carl Halbig died from the complications of a stroke. At the funeral procession almost all the employees and townspeople gave him a last farewell. His remains are buried in an urn in the park close to his house, next to the grave of his son Arno."

The Simon & Halbig porcelain factory made bisque-head dolls, all-bisque dolls and bisque parts for a large

CHAPTER 6

28. This 2-inch shoulder head has light-brown center-parted hair combed back from the face. The blue glass eyes are accented with upper and lower eyelashes. Unlike the majority of other Thuringian porcelain factories, the Simon & Halbig porcelain factory painted upper and lower eyelashes on most of their dollhouse dolls. The hair puffs in back are arranged on each side of a large braid. Ann Meehan Collection. (Photo: Curtis Haldy)

29. This 1½-inch shoulder head has beautifully painted eyes that include a heavy black outline around each iris. The dollhouse doll also has brush marks around the hairline and comb marks below the black headband. The darker red lip-accent line follows the curve of the upper lip to form the letter "M." Ann Meehan Collection. (Photo: Curtis Haldy)

30. This 6-inch bisque shoulder head marked "S10 H" has short curly brown hair, dark-brown glass eyes, multi-stroke eyebrows and upper and lower painted eyelashes. According to the Sonneberg museum's inventory card, this shoulder head was made in 1890 and donated to the museum by Simon & Halbig in 1910. Courtesy Deutsches Spielzeugmuseum, Sonneberg. (Photo: Christiane Gräfnitz)

number of German doll factories. The bisque quality is undeniable. The factory workers can be commended for the successful firing of the vast number and styles of doll heads made from 1869 until 1940.

Carl Halbig worked for the Alt, Beck & Gottschalck porcelain factory for many years. Therefore, it is not surprising that Alt, Beck & Gottschalck and Simon & Halbig parian-like shoulder heads are similar in modeling and facial painting. As is pointed out in the Ciesliks' 2001 *Puppenmagazin* article, Halbig took the Alt, Beck & Gottschalck porcelain recipes and the best workers with him when he moved with his wife (the widow Gottschalck) to Gräfenhain in 1868. The first doll-related porcelain was made a year later. It is only by grouping a number of shoulder heads made by a factory like Simon & Halbig that one can see the obvious similarities in modeling and painting. There are always slight differences in facial painting, but the modeling of the heads and attached shoulder plates is so similar that the "family" resemblance is apparent.

The facial painting details on Simon & Halbig parian-like shoulder heads differ from

31. For many years, the Simon & Halbig porcelain factory made a large number of dollhouse dolls. One identifiable facial feature is the long, individually painted upper and lower eyelashes. Small dolls made by other Thuringian porcelain factories seldom have upper and lower painted eyelashes. Other head features on this 6½-inch doll are center-parted hair, single-stroke eyebrows, glass eyes with upper and lower eyelashes, and a realistic mustache. Kathy and Mike Embry Collection. (Photo: Ann Hanat)

32. A black-ribbon headband, featuring an upside-down black bow, decorates the light-brown hairstyle on this 2½-inch shoulder head with center-parted short curly hair. The head features include lobe-pierced ears, blue glass eyes and upper and lower eyelashes. Margaret Hartshorn Collection. (Photo: Image Arts Etc.)

CHAPTER 6

33. The body on this original dollhouse doll with a 1½-inch shoulder head is very unusual. The un-tinted bisque shoulder plate has wire-strung moveable arms. The shoulder plate and arms are connected to a wood-and-leather center body section, as are the un-tinted bisque lower torso and attached legs. The lower legs have pink luster boots and white socks with a pink luster scalloped trim. The socks and shoes are identical to those molded and painted on the 3¾-inch Alice shown in illustration 26. The hat has a white luster feather trimmed in lavender. Ann Meehan Collection. (Photo: Curtis Haldy)

34. This dollhouse doll has a 1½-inch shoulder plate. It wears a tall gray hat and horseback-riding attire. Ann Meehan Collection. (Photo: Curtis Haldy)

35. This stylish Simon & Halbig shoulder-head doll wears a gray hat with an upturned brim. The black hatband features a large molded rosette. The head includes rare molded earrings and blue painted eyes with typical thick black upper-eyelid definition lines. Margaret Hartshorn Collection. (Photo: Image Arts Etc.)

36. This 1½-inch shoulder-head dollhouse doll has a well-modeled shoulder plate, long vertical curls, a large pink luster feather and a molded rose. Margaret Hartshorn Collection. (Photo: Image Arts Etc.)

37 This 6-inch wire-strung un-tinted bisque doll with a bald head has jointed arms only. The stationary legs have a very important identification feature: pink luster boots with matching pink sock edging in a scalloped pattern. Identical books with scalloped pink edging have been found on many other parian-like dolls made by this factory. The Alice-in-Wonderland dolls in illustrations 16 and 26 have the same painted details on the lower legs. Author's Collection. (Photo: Lee Krombholz)

38. This childlike 3½-inch turned shoulder head has facial modeling similar to that of the shoulder head in illustration 40. The head features include blue glass eyes, multi-stroke eyebrows and upper and lower eyelashes. Ten vertical curls are molded around the head. Margaret Hartshorn Collection. (Photo: Margaret Hartshorn)

39. This 3-inch shoulder head with glass eyes and side-parted hair is similar in facial modeling and painting to the shoulder head in illustration 38. Private Collection. (Photo: Margaret Hartshorn)

40. This childlike 4½-inch shoulder head has a swivel neck and a bow-tied black ribbon that holds the blond curly hair in place. An identical shoulder head in the Sonneberg museum was donated by Cuno & Otto Dressel in 1908. Margaret Hartshorn Collection. (Photo: Margaret Hartshorn)

41. The back hairstyle of the shoulder head seen in illustration 40 features eighteen vertical curls in varying lengths. Margaret Hartshorn Collection. (Photo: Margaret Hartshorn)

42.

43.

42. A dollhouse-size version of the doll in illustration 43 wears a large hat. The 1-inch shoulder head has detailed facial painting, blue glass eyes and well-painted upper and lower eyelashes. Ann Meehan Collection. (Photo: Curtis Haldy)

43. This 3-inch shoulder head has a full face, blue glass eyes, a cup-and-saucer swivel neck, multi-stroke eyebrows, upper and lower eyelashes and light-red lips. The center-parted hairstyle features loosely curled hair. Olson/Nelson Collection. (Photo: Red Kite Studios)

Alt, Beck & Gottschalck painting details in several ways. Simon & Halbig faces have thicker black lines outlining the upper eyelids; the mouths have an "M" shaped lip accent line that follows the curves of the upper lip; and, the upper lip is considerably larger. Also, Simon & Halbig parian-like shoulder heads usually have black iris outlines that completely encircle the iris.

Doll-related porcelain was the main product of the Simon & Halbig porcelain factory from 1869 until 1930, when it was directed by the Halbig family. A 1930 entry in the *German Doll Encyclopedia* reads: "Sole owner Kämmer & Reinhardt. Production: Bisque doll heads, export to all countries. Annual production 300,000 Reichsmark. 100 workers, 4 kilns. Director Ernst Rosenstock." The Simon & Halbig porcelain factory was torn down in the mid-1990s.

CHAPTER 6

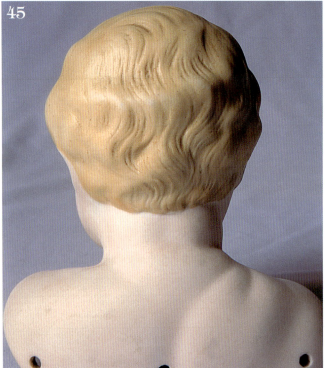

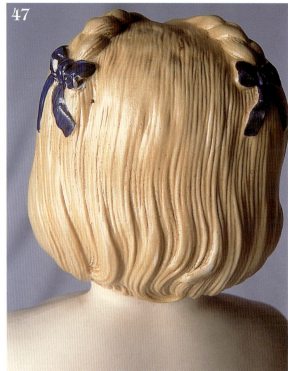

44. This turned-head boy doll with a side-parted hairstyle has a realistically modeled shoulder plate with underarm indentation lines that form a "V." Kenneth Drew Collection. (Photo: Ann Hanat)

45. The back view of the doll in illustration 44 shows the well-defined shoulder details. Kenneth Drew Collection. (Photo: Ann Hanat)

46. This blond-haired girl doll with a pensive expression has typical factory cheek blushing and a beautifully sculpted shoulder plate. Kenneth Drew Collection. (Photo: Ann Hanat)

47. The back hairstyle of the doll in illustration 46 features two braids tied with blue ribbons and deeply comb-marked hair. Kenneth Drew Collection. (Photo: Ann Hanat)

48. This boy doll has slightly wavy side-parted hair, fully outlined blue irises and generous cheek color. Olson/Nelson Collection. (Photo: Red Kite Studios)

49. Facial painting similar to that on the doll in illustration 47 is apparent on this boy doll with smoothly combed hair. Olson/Nelson Collection. (Photo: Red Kite Studios)

50. This 3¾-inch shoulder head is marked "S5H." The beautifully modeled and painted head has blue glass eyes, multi-stroke eyebrows and upper and lower eyelashes. The darker-red lip line follows the curve of the upper lip to form an "M." A shoulder head in the Sonneberg museum, dated 1875 by curators, was made from an identical master mold. Olson/Nelson Collection. (Photo: Red Kite Studios)

CHAPTER 7

Kestner & Co.

1. The sole remaining building that was once part of the Kestner & Co. porcelain factory is located close to the main town square in Ohrdruf. It is currently being used as a doctor's office. The Kestner factory sold doll-related porcelain products from the 1840s until the factory closed in 1938. (Photo: Mary Krombholz)

2. Doll collectors refer to this 4½-inch un-tinted bisque shoulder head as the Grape Lady because of the cluster of molded grapes decorating the white gold-trimmed snood ruffle on top of the head. The factory made many glazed porcelain examples of the Grape Lady, but parian-like examples are extremely rare. In my opinion, the Kestner factory made many more glazed-porcelain than unglazed-porcelain shoulder heads. Terry Schmeltzer Collection. (Photo: Estelle Johnston)

Johann Daniel Kestner, Jr., born the son of an innkeeper on September 4, 1784, had a major impact on dollmaking from his founding of a wooden-doll factory in Waltershausen in 1816 until his death on December 11, 1858. In September 2004, Christiane Gräfnitz verified with Thomas Reinecke, curator of the Museum Schloss (castle) Tenneberg in Waltershausen, that Kestner's 1824 doll factory is still standing on Neuengasse Street in Waltershausen today. The factory buildings cover a large portion of a block in the town, which was founded 775 years ago and has a current population of about 13,000.

Two years after Kestner's death, the Kestner doll factory purchased the Steudinger, Müller & Co. porcelain factory in Ohrdruf. While the Ciesliks note in their book *Puppen Sammeln* (Collecting Dolls), that "Kestner's books mention the first porcelain dolls after 1851," Christiane Gräfnitz, in her book titled *German Papier-Mâché Dolls: 1760-1860,* states that "In 1836, Kestner has dolls' porcelain

3. A dollhouse-doll version of the doll in illustration 5 has the same comb-marked hair and wide headband. The Kestner factory painted fine brush-strokes on the hairlines of many dollhouse dolls. The 6¼-inch doll has a 1½-inch shoulder head. Ann Meehan Collection. (Photo: Curtis Haldy)

4. This finely modeled example of a Kestner parian-like doll with an Alice-in-Wonderland hairstyle has a 5½-inch shoulder head with light-blond hair, brush marked at the hairline to include a widow's peak. A wide black headband holds the comb-marked hair in front and a black snood covers the hair in back. The facial features include long curving one-stroke eyebrows, painted eyes with a white iris highlight on the left side of each pupil and an unpainted space separating the lips. The white-iris highlights are in the same position as the eye highlights on shoulder heads pictured in the original 1860 Kestner sample pages in the Waltershausen Doll Museum. Olson/Nelson Collection. (Photo: Red Kite Studios)

5. Kestner made this 4½-inch un-tinted bisque shoulder head with a modified Flat Top comb-marked hairstyle. The long curving single-stroke eyebrows are typical of this porcelain factory. A second identification feature is the white highlight painted on the left side of each iris. The position of this highlight is identical to those found on the original 1860 sample sheets on display in the Museum Schloss Tenneberg in Waltershausen. A third important identification feature is the unpainted space between the upper and lower lips, which is especially visible directly between the upper lip peaks in this photo. Author's Collection. (Photo: Lee Krombholz)

6. This 4-inch parian-like shoulder head has a "cup-and-saucer" swivel neck, a separate square-cut shoulder plate, brown comb-marked hair, brown single-stroke eyebrows, white highlights painted on the left side of each iris and an unpainted space between the slightly smiling lips. The plain, comb-marked hairstyle has loosely curled hair in back. This head is similar in modeling and facial painting to several of the Kestner chinas pictured in my book titled *Identifying German Chinas, 1840s-1930s*. Andrea Jones Collection. (Photo: Andrea Jones)

7. The unusual 1850s shoulder-head doll shown in illustration 6 has a Taufling body with an un-tinted bisque shoulder plate, torso and lower limbs. The beautifully modeled forearms and lower legs with realistic bare feet are a credit to the Kestner sculptors. Andrea Jones Collection. (Photo: Andrea Jones)

8. This Kestner grandmother has center-parted gray molded hair styled with a bun in back. Margaret Hartshorn Collection. (Photo: Image Arts Etc.)

9. This 7-inch bald-headed grandfather has a brush-stroked fringe of hair over the ears and on the sides of the face. The large nose differs from the long thin noses of the soldiers and males with side-parted hair. The back shoulder plate contains a circular purple stamp that reads "Germany." Susan Moore Collection. (Photo: Digital Images)

10. Beautifully dressed parents and grandparents pose for a group photograph. Dollhouse dolls made from master molds identical to those used to make these four dolls are pictured in my 1918 Kestner sample book. Kathy and Mike Embry Collection. (Photo: Ann Hanat)

Chapter 7

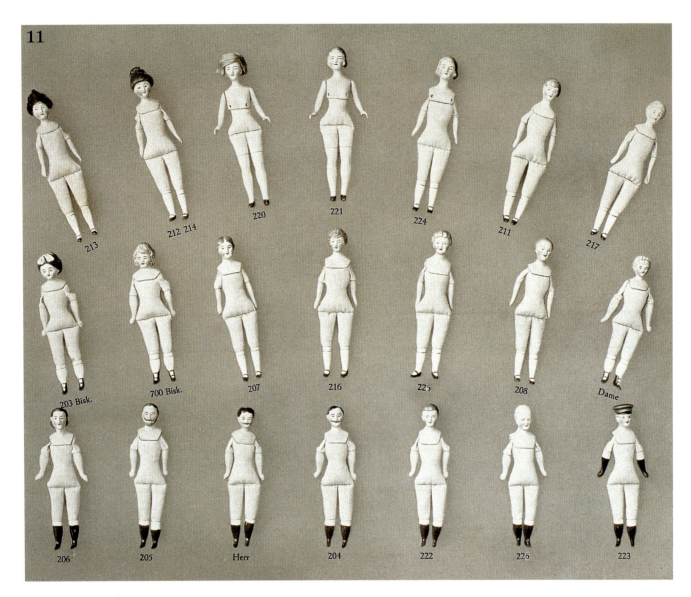

11. The Kestner & Co. porcelain factory made small parian-like play dolls for dollhouses from the 1860s until the 1930s. This page from my Kestner sample book of 1918 shows twenty-one undressed dollhouse dolls. The shoulder heads and lower limbs are made of un-tinted bisque. The shoulder heads receive pale or darker flesh-toned complexion coats before the facial features are painted. The lower legs in the sample-book photograph include boots, one- and two-strap shoes and simple oval-shaped shoes. It is possible to accurately date the sample book because the names of the three company directors are listed on the first page. Following the 1918 death of Adolf Kestner, the company was run by Ernst Bufe, Eduard Prechtl and Ernst Florschuetz. Sample books were often used for years after they were introduced. Author's Collection.

12. This group of Kestner dollhouse dolls is dressed in original military uniforms. The attention to detail on the bisque heads and clothing is apparent. The smaller dolls with molded mustaches are dressed in German-style military uniforms. Kathy and Mike Embry Collection. (Photo: Ann Hanat)

heads and limbs made in a factory, probably by the Müller Company in Ohrdurf." So while the factory did not purchase the Ohrdruf porcelain factory until 1860, it is assumed that the Müller or the Steudinger, Müller & Co. porcelain factory made early glazed porcelain doll heads for the Kestner doll factory.

The Museum Schloss Tenneberg contains an excellent collection of Kestner dolls. Along with the dolls, the museum owns a group of very important original factory sample books and dated documents. Thomas Reinecke does an excellent job of displaying the dolls and historical documents. The Museum Schloss Tenneberg has attributed seven glazed porcelain shoulder heads to the Kestner & Co. porcelain factory. The earliest china shoulder heads often have simple molded-bun hairstyles commonly worn by women in the 1840s. Therefore, we can date the Kestner dolls with buns to

this period of time. In my opinion, the Kestner porcelain factory made very few 1860s and 1870s parian-like dolls. They are easy to recognize because the facial painting details on the chinas and parian-like dolls are so similar, especially the unpainted space between the lips.

The Kestner porcelain factory in Ohrdruf produced a large number of dollhouse dolls. The fine quality of facial painting is evident on the six-to-nine-inch dolls. The faces of many of the dollhouse dolls include finely painted brush marks around the hairlines. Porcelain-factory painters spent many years serving as apprentice painters before they became proficient enough to paint more expensive porcelain products, like figurines and fine table ware. Dollhouse dolls and all-bisque dolls served as excellent teaching tools until an apprentice became an advanced painter.

Many Kestner dollhouse shoulder heads were made of un-tinted bisque, however dollhouse shoulder heads were also made of flesh-tinted bisque. Once bisque heads had been fired and thoroughly sanded, artists were ready to apply tinting (a complexion coat). In her book titled *All-Bisque and Half-Bisque Dolls*, author Genevieve Angione describes the application of a doll's complexion coat in the following way: "A wad of lamb's wool enclosed by a piece of China silk is used to 'pad' the color to an even, streak-less state of perfection. This takes a bit of doing because as the silk and wool absorb the excess paint, it can be transferred to a previously finished area." Following the application of a complexion coat, the head was allowed to dry completely before the facial features were painted. The head was also air-dried between each step of the eyebrow, eye and mouth painting, to prevent smearing of the colors.

After the porcelain shoulder heads were kiln-fired to

13. This parian-like dollhouse doll is marked with the mold number "514" and the size number "10/0." The tan comb-marked hairstyle features two molded curls on the forehead. The Kestner dollhouse dolls in illustrations 14 and 15 are wearing the same type of heeled boot as the one pictured on the sample page. The boots end at the knees on the male doll and at the ankle on this lady doll. This doll is also pictured with four others in the Introduction. Author's Collection. (Photo: Red Kite Studios)

14. This 7¼-inch parian-like male dollhouse doll is dressed in formal morning dress, consisting of a black felt cutaway jacket and striped wool pants. White paper is inserted under the black vest to simulate a shirt and high collar. The tan side-parted hair has well-defined comb marks in back. The back shoulder plate is incised with the mold number "529" and a size number. Author's Collection. (Photo: Red Kite Studios)

15. A 7-inch Kestner bisque dollhouse doll is dressed in an original military uniform consisting of a red felt jacket, black felt pants and black oilcloth knee boots. The jacket and pants are elaborately trimmed with gold-embossed paper. Accessories include a red gold-trimmed shield and a realistic curved metal sword with a gold handle. In 1892, an identical doll sold in a New York City toy store for 48 cents. Author's Collection. (Photo: Red Kite Studios)

16. This closer view of the doll in Illustration 15 shows the single-stroke eyebrows, blue painted eyes and large molded and painted mustache. The dark-blond hairstyle has finely painted brush-marked hair around the hairline. Author's Collection. (Photo: Red Kite Studios)

17. This bisque chauffeur with a 1½-inch shoulder head stands out on the lower right corner of the Kestner 1918 sample-book page because of the molded hat and unusual driving glasses. Kathy and Mike Embry Collection. (Photo: Ann Hanat)

make the facial colors permanent, home workers mounted them on cloth or kid bodies, then dressed them. The home workers, who included children, were a very important part of the Thuringian work force for hundreds of years. From the book titled *Reise ins Spielzeugland* (A Journey in Toyland) by Marion Cristiana Müller we learn that that the Kestner doll factory had 1,264 workers in 1846 and that, of this number, 423 were children younger than fourteen. In 1890, the Kestner doll factory had between 500 and 600 home workers.

According to the Ciesliks' research, as noted in their *German Doll Encyclopedia*, it was not until 1904 that the German government enacted an "Act on the Work of Children." From this date on, Thuringian children from the age of eight years on were allowed to do the following jobs: "Painting and brushing of doll joints; sorting and inserting of doll eyes; blowing of doll eyes by bellows; sewing, crocheting and knitting of doll dresses; sewing doll bodies; making curls for the doll wigs as long as cleaned hair of wool or mohair was used; and packing the dolls in paper boxes."

Kestner sample books provide accurate information on the porcelain products made by this Thuringian factory. I was fortunate to have the opportunity to buy an original Kestner sample book a few years ago. The front cover includes a raised gold crown with the following words: "Kronen Puppen" (King Dolls), and the name Kestner underneath. Below the crown are the following words: "J.D. Kestner, jun. Puppenfabrik (doll factory) and Kestner & Comp. Porzellanfabrik (porcelain factory)." The first page of the sample book contains a group picture of the buildings that once made up the porcelain factory site. Only one building remains from the original porcelain factory site. The two-story building now houses a doctor's office.

The original Kestner sample book contains thirty-two pages of color as well as black-and-white photographs of the company's doll-related porcelain and doll accessories. Following the pictures of bisque head dolls on composition bodies, the book shows wigged and molded-hair half-dolls, all-bisque dolls, dollhouse dolls and bisque socket heads without bodies. Following the page of composition bodies, the sample book includes a page of doll wigs in a variety of styles. Doll clothing and shoes are also pictured. The bisque-head googlies and other character dolls pictured in the sample book are very collectible today.

The Ciesliks' research in the *German Doll Encyclopedia* helps date this sample book by listing the names of the men who directed the Kestner doll and porcelain factory in 1918, following the death of Adolf Kestner, J.D. Kestner's grandson, the same year. The three directors, Ernst Bufe, Eduard Prechtl and Ernst Florschuet, are also listed under the photograph of the porcelain factory in my sample book. From this sample book, we are able to identify a group of Kestner dolls and accessories made shortly after World War I. Porcelain factories pictured the same top-selling products in succeeding sample books for many years.

The Kestner porcelain factory closed in 1938, marking the end of a dollmaking era that had begun 122 years earlier. From the introduction of lathe-turned wooden dolls in 1816 to the last porcelain dolls made after World War I, the Kestner factory produced the largest variety of dolls of the finest quality, surpassing the work of all other porcelain and doll factories in Thuringia. The standards this company set encouraged other doll and porcelain factories to strive to produce work of equivalent quality. The trademark crown of superiority on the front of the 1824 factory building still glitters in the sunlight, serving as a reminder of the millions of fine dolls produced there for more than a century.

18. This 5½-inch all-bisque doll is dressed in an original ethnic costume representing the Alsace-Lorraine region of France. The tiny one-stroke surprised eyebrows, side-glancing eyes, button nose and watermelon-slice mouth create an impish expression. Susan Moore Collection. (Photo: Digital Images)

19. These two all-bisque dolls, measuring 5 and 5½ inches, are identical to those in the illustrations in my Kestner sample book from 1918. Max is the round-faced black-haired boy with finely painted brushstrokes around the forehead and an impish mouth. Moritz is the red-haired boy with a distinctive hairstyle, featuring a curled top knot. Both dolls have side-glancing eyes. Cartoonist William Busch created these mischievous boys in 1858 for his first cartoons. His book describing their many exploits was published in 1865 and translated into English in 1870. Kathy and Mike Embry Collection. (Photo: Ann Hanat)

20. These 3½-inch all-bisque bride and groom Kewpie "Huggers" are dressed in original crepe-paper clothing. The bride is wearing the remnants of an original net veil headpiece. The groom is wearing an original crepe-paper tuxedo jacket and top hat. The bare feet with well-defined toes are painted black to simulate shoes. The small blue wings and starfish hands are excellent identification guides. Author's Collection. (Photo: Red Kite Studios)

21. This page from an original 1918 Kester & Co. porcelain factory sample book pictures the all-bisque dolls Max and Moritz. The two dolls are shown with fifty-eight other all-bisque dolls on page 61 of my book titled *German Porcelain Dolls, 1836-2002*. They have mischievous expressions created by the sculpted and painted facial features. Author's Collection.

Chapter 8

Hertwig & Co.

The Hertwig & Co. porcelain factory was founded in the town of Katzhütte, Thuringia in 1864. The German word Katzhütte translates as "cat hut." Many of the figurines made by this factory bear the symbol of a cat on a roof. The large factory site, made up of many buildings that varied in age and construction style, was leveled to the ground in 2004. The only building still standing on the factory site has an octagonal turret on the roof. It is pictured in illustration 1.

For many years, Hertwig parian-like shoulder heads have been described as "stone bisque dolls." This name, a misnomer, in my opinion, has stuck. The word "stone" in the term refers to the gray-like stone color of the porcelain. Doll-related porcelain made by the Hertwig factory is stark white, however, rather than gray-white. Japanese copies of German porcelain products, on the other hand, often do have a gray cast. I believe early collectors may have mixed these dolls up with the Japanese copies that were made from German molds, particularly from Hertwig molds.

A study of the original Hertwig sample boards in the Sonneberg Doll Museum contradicts the descriptions

1. The Hertwig & Co. porcelain factory was located in the Thuringian town of Katzhütte. The factory buildings varied in age and construction style. All the buildings on the factory site were demolished in 2004, with the exception of the white building on the left in this photograph. (Photo: Mary Krombholz)

2. Eight head shards wear a variety of molded hats. They show the fine pastel facial painting found on dolls of high quality made by this factory beginning in 1865. Author's Collection. (Photo: Gene Abbott)

3. The facial modeling and painting on this shoulder head found on the sample board is similar to that on the shoulder-head shard in the top right corner of illustration 2. The special features include a large ruffled hat, a molded blouse with a gold-trimmed pink bow and a blue gold-edged vest. Courtesy Dr. Christopher Hertwig and Deutsches Spielzeugmuseum, Sonneberg. (Photo: Christiane Gräfnitz)

offered by authors and doll collectors as to the poor quality of the glazed and unglazed shoulder heads made by this factory. The modeling and painting of the shoulder heads still tied to original sample boards is as fine as that of the porcelain shoulder heads made by any other Thuringian porcelain factory. The quality of painting may not be as fine on the dolls that originally sold for lower prices, but the dolls of top quality have finely textured bisque and beautiful facial painting.

Chapter 8

4. This important 1900 Hertwig sample board in the doll museum in Sonneberg is on loan from Dr. Christopher Hertwig, who inherited the sample board from his father, Ernst Friedrich Hertwig. It has nineteen hatted and bonneted shoulder heads still tied to the original board. Thirteen individual shoulder heads on the sample board were photographed by Christiane Gräfnitz in March 2004. They are pictured in illustrations 3, 5, 6, 7, 8, 9, 11, 12, 13, 14, 15, 16 and 17. They show the fine un-tinted bisque and facial painting of shoulder heads sold under the description "better quality." I am grateful to Dr. Christopher Hertwig and the Sonneberg Doll Museum for allowing me to publish the photographs of the thirteen sample board shoulder heads. Courtesy Dr. Christopher Hertwig and Deutsches Spielzeugmuseum, Sonneberg. (Photo: Christiane Gräfnitz)

Hertwig & Co.

5. This Hertwig shoulder head wears a large turned-up hat brim trimmed with a large orange bow and streamers. The V-neck blouse includes ruffles and an orange painted decoration. Courtesy Dr. Christopher Hertwig and Deutsches Spielzeugmuseum, Sonneberg. (Photo: Christiane Gräfnitz)

6. The main feature of this parian-like shoulder head is a large molded hat with a large triangular-shaped ruffle. A feather is molded over the top edge of the hat. The gathered ruffle under the brim and large bow on each side of the hat are added decorations. The high-necked unpainted blouse includes tucks and eyelet trim. The head features include blond shoulder-length hair, painted eyes and generously blushed cheeks. Courtesy Dr. Christopher Hertwig and Deutsches Spielzeugmuseum, Sonneberg. (Photo: Christiane Gräfnitz)

7. This light-blue bonnet has two separate ruffles and a decorative ruffle under the hat brim. A pink bow with gold streamers is molded under the chin. Head features include blond bangs, molded eyelids and a pouty mouth. Courtesy Dr. Christopher Hertwig and Deutsches Spielzeugmuseum, Sonneberg. (Photo: Christiane Gräfnitz)

Chapter 8

8. The beautifully molded and painted details on this shoulder head with a black face include a realistic "knitted" bonnet edged in realistic pink "fur" and tied with a yellow bow. Matching pink trim decorates the blouse, which is styled with gold beads that are molded in an intricate diamond-shaped pattern. This shoulder head was also made with a white face. Courtesy Dr. Christopher Hertwig and Deutsches Spielzeugmuseum, Sonneberg. (Photo: Christiane Gräfnitz)

9. This cone-shaped hat is decorated with a pink scalloped band and a dark blue bow. The long blond hairstyle resembles the hairstyles shown in illustrations 5 and 6. A special molded feature is the large gold cross necklace. Courtesy Dr. Christopher Hertwig and Deutsches Spielzeugmuseum, Sonneberg. (Photo: Christiane Gräfnitz)

10. A blue molded bow trims the elaborate ruffled, pink-trimmed bonnet on this 18-inch parian-like doll. A white triangular bow-trimmed insert under the brim is molded in an intricate pattern. Courtesy Deutsches Spielzeugmuseum, Sonneberg. (Photo: Christiane Gräfnitz)

11. Raised molded flowers decorate the straw-like bonnet with an upturned brim and a blue bow that ties under the chin. The painted flowers and raised dots on the hat brim varied in color and quality of hand-painted details. Courtesy Dr. Christopher Hertwig and Deutsches Spielzeugmuseum, Sonneberg. (Photo: Christiane Gräfnitz)

12. This unusual Hertwig shoulder head has a large molded bow painted the same color as the hair. The round face is similar in modeling to the bald head shown in illustration 31. A gold molded comb decorates the hairstyle. Courtesy Deutsches Spielzeugmuseum, Sonneberg. (Photo: Christiane Gräfnitz)

It is evident that more of the later dolls are poorly finished and painted, especially those made after World War I. In fact, the shoulder heads can be separated into two groups: those made in smaller numbers during the first thirty-five years of production, and those made from approximately 1900 on. The style of painting is very different and the quality of earlier dolls is very apparent. A larger percentage of the millions of shoulder head made from 1900 on are more likely to be poorly sanded and painted. As is true for many other Thuringian porcelain factories, the same head molds were used to make figurines and doll heads.

Florence Theriault's 2000 book titled *Hertwig & Co. Archives, 1890-1937* is an excellent identification guide to the factory's doll-related porcelain products. The 136-page book is filled with color and black-and-white pictures of original sample boards and factory products. Theriault uses the information in original sample books to provide accurate descriptions of the dolls on the sample boards.

CHAPTER 8

13. This expressive shoulder head with molded eyelids and glazed pupils wears a blue hat trimmed with a large rosette and gold decoration. The top of the scoop-necked blouse is edged with a ruffle and gold beads. A gold locket hangs from the blue ribbon necklace. The facial painting is an example of the earlier style of facial painting, with finely painted blond hair, eyes, single-stroke eyebrows and mouth. Courtesy Dr. Christopher Hertwig and Deutsches Spielzeugmuseum, Sonneberg. (Photo: Christiane Gräfnitz)

14. This beautiful example of a Hertwig parian-like shoulder head has a molded upswept blond hairstyle trimmed with pink flowers and pink leaves. The blouse collar is outlined with gold beads. The front opening, bow and buttons are painted bright gold. Courtesy Dr. Christopher Hertwig and Deutsches Spielzeugmuseum, Sonneberg. (Photo: Christiane Gräfnitz)

One group of shoulder-head boys with blue bows is pictured on page twenty of Theriault's book. The caption reads: "Sample Box of Bisque Charakter-Puppen. Boys with Blue Bow Ties.... shown in the 1914 Hertwig 50th Anniversary Catalog as model 217, from 'better series', offered in twelve sizes, and at twice the cost of fancier bonnet-head dolls in that same catalog." Shoulder heads made from identical master molds are shown in illustrations 23 and 24.

The words "better series" aptly describes the difference in quality of the dolls made and offered for sale by this factory. The quality of modeling and painting varied considerably depending on the price per doll a buyer was willing to pay. The price lists in many of my original Thuringian porcelain factory sample books offer the customer a choice of quality on each article. The Hertwig porcelain factory sold large amounts of doll-related porcelain to the New York importers Butler Brothers from 1877 on. The Butler Brothers Company acted as middlemen between the porcelain factory and American

wholesale buyers. Mail-order houses, department stores and "five and dime" stores across the country clamored for inexpensive, attractive dolls. Hertwig parian-like dolls were very popular with buyers because the price per doll was low and the appeal was high. Hertwig dolls described as "stone bisque" dolls are often the factory's hatted and bonneted shoulder heads, which were made in large numbers for several decades. John Noble paints an excellent word picture of these dolls in his 1971 book titled *A Treasury of Beautiful Dolls*. Noble writes: "These dolls were known in contemporary print as hooded chinas or fancies. One series that wore flowers or insects as headgear were described as Marguerite Dolls. They are, of course, the descendants of the above-mentioned fancy-bisque dolls, but they are different from their antecedents. For one thing, they are a much poorer product, for the bisque itself is coarse and heavy. They have more in common with the dolls made of candy that used to be sold at Christmas time. They have the same sugariness and, for all the slapdash bravura, a transitory look, as though they were not meant to last."

Home workers were a very important part of the Hertwig factory's success, as they were for many doll and porcelain factories. In the *German Doll Encyclopedia*, the Ciesliks describe Hertwig home workers in 1888: "600 workers, most of them in home-trade are employed for sewing, stuffing and finishing the production. By this method they produced in summer 1000 to 1200 and in winter 2000 dozen dolls per day." When collectors criticize the quality of the bisque and the facial painting on many Hertwig glazed and un-glazed dolls, we must remember that porcelain workers were not required to sand and paint inexpensive dolls as carefully as the higher-priced dolls.

15. This parian-like shoulder head wears an unpainted hat with a flat brim trimmed with a very large bow. The unpainted blouse has a high collar, eyelet trim and a molded bow. Only the facial features and long blond hair are painted. Courtesy Dr. Christopher Hertwig and Deutsches Spielzeugmuseum, Sonneberg. (Photo: Christiane Gräfnitz)

16. The two sections of this large molded hat are separated by a turquoise band. The blouse has a large pale-turquoise bow and a high collar molded over the chin. The light-brown hair is styled with horizontal curls covering the ears. Courtesy Dr. Christopher Hertwig and Deutsches Spielzeugmuseum, Sonneberg. (Photo: Christiane Gräfnitz)

Chapter 8

17. Blue and black sections create a checkerboard effect on this bonnet with a large up-turned brim. A blue bow decorates the bonnet, while a second large bow with streamers holds the hat in place. Bonnets and hats differ; bonnets have ties while hats do not. Courtesy Dr. Christopher Hertwig and Deutsches Spielzeugmuseum, Sonneberg. (Photo: Christiane Gräfnitz.)

18. The shoulder head on the far right of illustration 19 is wearing a blue-trimmed butterfly hat similar to this pink-painted example. The realistic butterfly body and antenna are molded on top of the head between the colorful wings on these so-called Marguerite Dolls. Author's Collection. (Photo: Red Kite Studios)

19. These four parian-like shoulder heads were advertised as Marguerite Dolls. According to *The Collector's Encyclopedia of Dolls, Volume I,* by the Colemans, Butler Brothers sold the dolls in 1905 as "fancy bonnet heads with china limbs and cloth bodies; size 7¾-inch, priced 37 cents a dozen, wholesale." They were advertised using the names "cloverleaf, butterfly and flower designed" hats. As can be expected, painting quality decreased on parian-like dolls that originally sold for pennies. Author's Collection. (Photo: Gene Abbott)

Hertwig & Co.

20. This blue "knitted" cone-shaped hat has a white band that is tied in a bow with three long streamers. The blond hairstyle has a curl molded over the hat in front. Margaret Hartshorn Collection. (Photo: Image Arts Etc.)

21. A 7-inch parian-like Frozen Charlotte has long, curly center-parted hair and a towering hat decorated with shades of blue and tied with a large pink molded bow. The back of the unpainted bonnet has a ruffle molded onto the shoulders. The molded white socks and blue shoes are well painted. Margaret Hartshorn Collection. (Photo: Image Arts Etc.)

22. This 7¾-inch un-tinted Hertwig parian-like bust is painted with the soft pastel colors that resemble the shoulder-head shards in illustration 2. The open mouth with painted teeth is similar in modeling and painting to the photograph of two busts and a shoulder head shown in the Introduction. Author's Collection. (Photo: Gregg Smith)

CHAPTER 8

23. A shoulder head made from the same master mold as the boy on the sample board is pictured with an equally well-painted and modeled girl. The boy is pictured in the Hertwig 1914 Fiftieth Anniversary Catalog. The model number is 217, from the "better series." According to *Hertwig & Co Archives, 1890-1937* by Florence Theriault, the shoulder-head doll was priced higher than hatted and bonneted shoulder heads. The girl portrays an older child. The blond side-parted hair features a large pink bow. The blouse has a ruffled collar with blue edging. Susan Moore Collection. (Photo: Digital Images)

24. This pair of Hertwig shoulder heads with original nanking bodies and parian-like lower limbs, are tied to another sample board in the Sonneberg Museum owned by Dr. Christopher Hertwig. The blond-haired boys with pensive expressions have large blue molded bows molded on their shoulder plates. Courtesy Deutsches Spielzeugmuseum, Sonneberg. (Photo: Christiane Gräfnitz)

25. A shoulder-head doll with side-glancing eyes and a nanking body with parian-like lower limbs is still tied in the lower right corner of an original Hertwig sample board. This sample board is owned by Sophie Berlinger, daughter of Hans Hertwig. I am grateful to Frau Berlinger for allowing me to include the sample board in this chapter. Courtesy Deutsches Spielzeugmuseum, Sonneberg. (Photo: Christiane Gräfnitz)

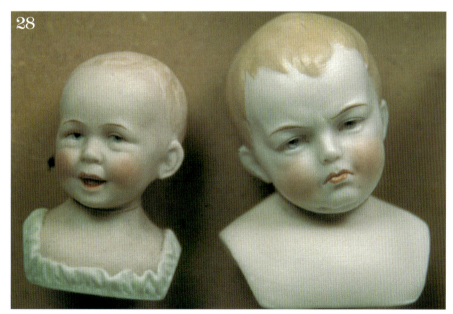

26. This pre-tinted shoulder head was made from a mold identical to the one used for the doll on the sample board shown in illustration 25. It is marked with the trademark Hertwig "Germany," in which the "G" has a downward curving line and the "y" has a curl at the end of the straight tail. The head with a bobbed hairstyle has reddish-blond hair with well-defined comb marks and a surprised expression. It is pictured in the Hertwig 1914 Fiftieth Anniversary Catalog as model 365. It was made in thirteen sizes. Author's Collection. (Photo: Red Kite Studios)

27. The unusual open/closed mouth on this shoulder head has upper and lower painted teeth. Short curly blond hair frames the expressive chubby-cheeked face. Courtesy Dr. Christopher Hertwig and Deutsches Spielzeugmuseum, Sonneberg. (Photo: Christiane Gräfnitz)

28. These two character boys have unusual laughing and crying expressions molded on their well-sculpted character faces. The shoulder head on the left has a ruffled shoulder plate. Courtesy Dr. Christopher Hertwig and Deutsches Spielzeugmuseum, Sonneberg. (Photo: Christiane Gräfnitz)

In the late 1990s, following the closing of the Hertwig factory, sales tables at the annual Neustadt Puppenfestival were filled with Hertwig parian-like shoulder-head shards with molded hair, hats and bonnets. They were inexpensive, therefore I bought hundreds of them. They are fascinating to study because they show the wide range of small modeling variations that changed the appearance of each shoulder head.

It is difficult to date the factory's parian-like dolls with any certainty. A German collector who owns an original Hertwig

CHAPTER 8

29. This row of Hertwig dollhouse dolls is still tied to a sample board in the doll museum in Sonneberg, owned by Dr. Christopher Hertwig. The doll on the left side of the row is dressed in a maid's black uniform with a white apron. Courtesy Deutsches Spielzeugmuseum, Sonneberg. (Photo: Christiane Gräfnitz)

30. This Hertwig dollhouse doll has a molded hat identical to the one on the doll on the sample board, but wears slightly different original clothing. Courtesy Margaret Hartshorn. (Photo: Image Arts Etc)

31. This bald parian-like shoulder head is tied to another sample board in the Sonneberg Doll Museum owned by Dr. Christopher Hertwig. The facial features are finely painted and include unusual multi-stroke eyebrows. The unpainted pate and realistically molded shoulders are special features of this shoulder head. Two other shoulder heads still tied to this board are shown in illustrations 27 and 28. Courtesy Deutsches Spielzeugmuseum, Sonneberg. (Photo: Christiane Gräfnitz)

32. This 7-inch un-tinted bisque doll has jointed arms, stationary legs and pink shoes with two straps and heels. The ribbed white socks are banded in blue. The bald head has a single large hole on the crown. Important facial identification features are the single-stroke eyebrows and large irises without any outline or hightlight. These painted details are typical of the majority of dolls made by this factory. The eyebrows are painted in a wrap-around fashion, partially encircling the eye below. The hands are well modeled with excellent finger definition. The back of the torso is marked with the incised mold number "2235" and the large size number "8." Author's Collection. (Photo: Lee Krombholz)

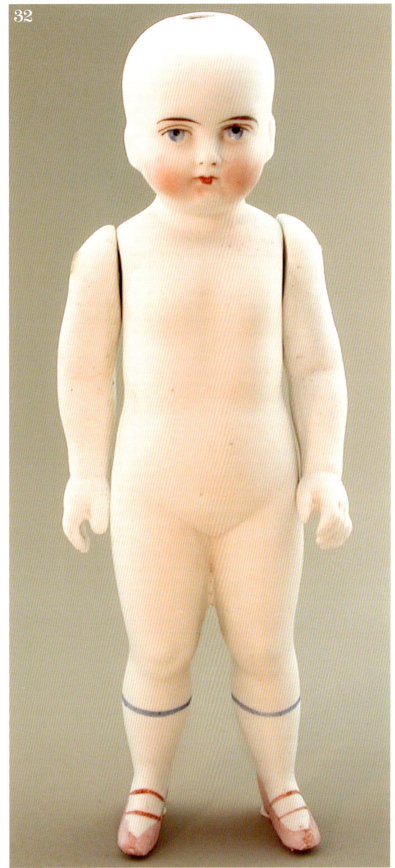

factory ledger notes that doll heads are listed in an 1865 entry, a year after the factory was founded. Many of the shards in my collection are examples of the earliest type of facial painting. The shards are made of fine-textured bisque and the painting of the gray-brown hair and pastel facial features is excellent.

The early parian-like shoulder heads and figurines made by the factory are very similar in modeling and facial painting. It is often difficult to tell if a doll-head shard was part of a figurine or a doll unless the shoulder plate is partially intact. An early figurine displayed in the Town Museum in Katzhütte has the same type of facial painting as many of my early shards.

The eight early head shards pictured in illustration 2 are good examples of the earliest dolls, although the shards were buried for over a hundred years. Porcelain doll-head shards have staying power. They can be exposed to extreme heat or freezing temperatures and never change. They can rest on an ocean floor for decades in a sunken ship, and when they are brought to the surface, the facial painting is remarkably intact. Documented shards are our best source of

CHAPTER 8

33. These eleven Hertwig all-bisque dolls, circa 1920, are made of pre-tinted bisque. They measure from 2 to 3 inches in height. The dolls in the top row wear original clothing. Author's Collection. (Photo: Gene Abbott)

34. This pre-tinted all-bisque doll with side-glancing eyes and a dimpled chubby body is marked "359-4" on the back shoulders. In December of 1925, similar examples cost 84 cents a dozen in the Butler Brothers Wholesale Catalog. Author's Collection. (Photo: Red Kite Studios)

irrefutable evidence of past production. They teach us that each Thuringian porcelain factory used a painting style and colors that were unique to that factory. If doll collectors could study the beautiful parian-like Hertwigs hanging on the original sample boards in the Sonneberg Museum, they would understand that Hertwig made parian-like dolls that are equal in quality to those made at the Kestner, Kister and ABG porcelain factories.

When the Hertwig & Co. porcelain factory site was leveled a few years ago, many important artifacts relating to the company disappeared from view. I had the rare opportunity to tour the buildings in 1999. Although the porcelain contents had been removed, many permanent features remained to remind one of the years when factory employees made doll-related porcelain in Katzhütte.

Each building reflected the work that once took place inside. One of the most interesting had an area for the production of cloth doll bodies and clothing. The most graphic reminders of the work once carried out here were the lines of large holes in the old wooden floor, which once held bolts that kept dozens of sewing machines in

place. Next to this area was a large wooden shelving unit, which still contained small cardboard patterns for making simple doll dresses. Another building, used by artists, modelers and photographers, had the black-out shades, meant to keep out the light during photography sessions, still attached to the large windows. Transfer patterns were neatly stacked in one cabinet. Some contained floral patterns used for tableware; others featured unusual medallions.

My favorite building was the one where plaster molds were created and stored. The mold storage shelves were supported by slim tree saplings. A few molds were still stored on a balcony. In the attic a ten-foot wooden table, with a well-designed scrolled top, was identified by a cardboard placard as having been used to display Hertwig porcelain products at the 1926 Leipzig Fair.

Although physical traces of the old Hertwig porcelain factory have disappeared, the porcelain products made in Katzhütte from 1864 until 1990 are on display in museum and private doll collections worldwide. It is well worth visiting the Katzhütte Town Museum to see the outstanding collection of factory catalogs and exceptional porcelain figurines.

35. These two Hertwig all-bisque dolls, measuring 4 inches and 6½ inches, are made from master molds similar to the one used to make the doll pictured in illustration 36. The unglazed porcelain was not well sanded or painted on either doll, and so the dolls sold for a lower price than the finer example, although the molds were the same. Author's Collection. (Photo: Kirtley Krombholz)

36. This all-bisque curly-haired 5½-inch boy is typical of the fine quality found on many of the wire-strung jointed dolls made by this factory. The molded clothing includes a white "knitted" sweater and hat, knee-length pants, long white socks and painted shoes. The realistic hands are slightly curled. The back of the pink molded pants are incised with the mold number "145G." The intaglio eyes are a special modeling feature. Courtesy Andrea Jones. (Photo: Andrea Jones)

Conclusion

The years have not been kind to the porcelain factories that once made dolls and toys in this picturesque area of Germany. The Thuringian mountains surround the villages that nestle in the valleys. The red tile roofs are visible for miles as the narrow roads lead up through the vast forests of pine and spruce trees. Because entire families worked at the same factory for generation after generation, the closing of a porcelain factory had a major impact on a village.

With each passing year, German doll researchers are less likely to find original sources relating to porcelain production. It is fortunate that many doll-head shards were buried under the floorboards in old porcelain factories. The dumping grounds are also filled with doll treasures from the past.

Very few porcelain factories exist today and every year it becomes harder to find traces of the dollmaking past. Yet, although the majority of Thuringian porcelain factories are closed today, information concerning doll-related porcelain products continues to surface. By studying porcelain shards, ephemera and oral histories such as those documented in this book, we can continue to learn about the dolls we so avidly collect today.

Please see page 47 for details.

Glossary

Bisque or biscuit: unglazed porcelain

Blouse: a loose upper garment worn by women and children as part of their outer clothing

Bodice: the part of a woman's dress covering the body between the neck or shoulders and the waist

Bonnet: a covering for the head usually tied under the chin with strings or ribbons

Burning: firing porcelain

Chemise: a woman's loose-fitting shirt-like undergarment

China: glazed porcelain

Collar: the part of a shirt, coat, dress or blouse that encompasses the neckline of a garment, sewed so that it can fold or roll over. It is worn around the neck or at the neckline of a garment.

Dress: an outer garment for women and girls, consisting of a bodice and skirt in one piece

Giesschlicker: German word referring to the completed casting slip that was poured into plaster working molds

Googly eyes: eyes glancing to the side, whether painted or glass inset

Hat: a shaped covering for the head, usually with a crown and brim

Kaolin: fine white clay used for making porcelain, named for Kao-ling, a hill in southeast China where the first kaolin was dug

Luster: a metallic decoration derived chemically from gold or platinum in solution for use with porcelain. The English spelling of the word is "lustre."

Masse: German term used to refer to the porcelain mixture that forms slip that was poured into the plaster working molds

Parian-like dolls: dolls made of fine white bisque without tinting or with very slight tinting

Porcelain: a hard white nonporous translucent variety of ceramic ware made of kaolin, quartz and feldspar that was fired in a kiln to fuse the elements

Porcelain mixture: a combination of kaolin, quartz and feldspar mixed together to form slip so that it can be poured into molds; referred to in German as masse

Portrait dolls: dolls having facial characteristics identifiable with a particular person

Ruche: a strip of pleated lace, net, muslin, or other material for trimming or finishing a dress, as at the collar or sleeves

Schamotte: a fireproof ceramic container used to protect objects during kiln firing

Sekerkegel: small slim pyramic-shaped cones used to indicate different melting points from 600 to 2000 degrees Centigrade

Sharfbrenner: German word for "sharp" or extremely high firing

Shirt: a long-or short-sleeved garment for the upper part of the body, usually lightweight and having a collar and a front opening

Slip: term used to refer to clay to which water has been added to give it the consistency of cream so that it can easily by poured into a mold

Tint: a shade of color; a delicate or pale color; (as verb) to color slightly

Turner: a German worker who was responsible for removing porcelain products from plaster molds and trimming excess porcelain from the mold seams

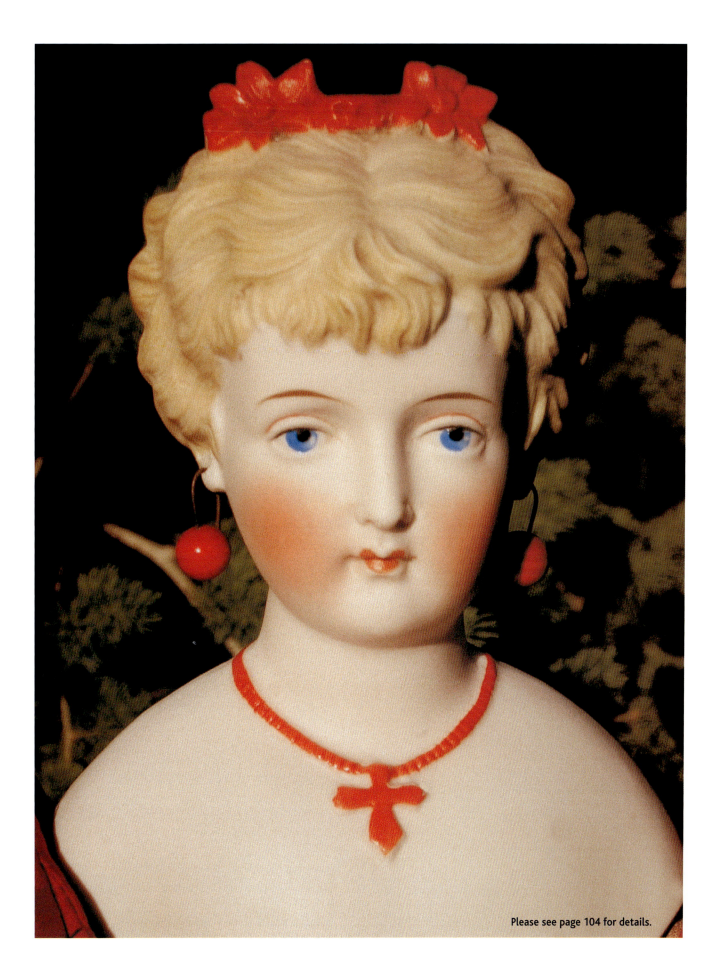

Please see page 104 for details.

Bibliography

Aldridge, Eileen. *Porcelain, A Grosset All-Color Guide*. New York: Grosset & Dunlap, Inc., 1970.

Angione, Genevieve. *All-Bisque and Half-Bisque Dolls*. Exon, PA: Schiffer Publishing Ltd., 1969.

_____. *Simon & Halbig – Master Craftsman. Spinning Wheels's Complete Book of Dolls*. New York: Galahad Books, 1949-1975.

_____ and Whorton, Judith. *All Dolls Are Collectible*. Annapolis, MD: Gold Horse Publishing, 1977, 1983.

Battie, David. *Sotheby's Concise Encyclopedia of Porcelain*. London: Conrad Octopus Limited, 1990, 1994 and 1995.

Borger, Mona. *Chinas, Dolls for Study and Admiration*. San Francisco: Borger Publications, 1983.

Bristol Olivia. *Dolls, A Collector's Guide*. London: De Agostini Editions, 1997.

Bullard, Helen and Callicot, Catherine. "Kestner Dolls from the 1890s to the 1920s." *Spinning Wheel's Complete Book of Dolls*. New York: Galahad Books, 1949-1975.

Cieslik, Juergen and Marianne. *German Doll Encyclopedia, 1800-1939*: Cumberland, MD: Hobby House Press, Inc., 1985.

_____. *German Doll Marks and Identification Book*. Annapolid, MD: Gold Horse Publishing, 2001.

_____. *German Doll Studies*. Annapolis, MD: Gold Horse Publishing, 1999.

_____. *Puppen Sammeln*. Munich: Emil Vollmer, 1980.

Coleman, Dorothy S. *Prices for Dolls*. Riverdale, MD: Hobby House Press, 1977.

_____, Elizabeth Ann and Evelyn Jane. *The Collector's Book of Dolls' Clothes, Costumes in Miniature, 1700-1929*. New York: Crown Publishers, Inc., 1975.

_____. *The Collector's Encyclopedia of Dolls*. New York: Crown Publishers, Inc., 1968.

_____. *The Collector's Encyclopedia of Dolls, Volume Two*. New York: Crown Publishers, Inc., 1986.

Copper, Emanuel. *Ten Thousand Years of Pottery*. Philadelphia, PA: University of Pennsylvania Press, 1972, 1981, 1988 and 2000.

Cooper, Marlow. *Dimples and Sawdust*. Privately published, no date.

_____ and Van Kampen, Dee. *Dimples and Sawdust, Volume Two*. Privately published, 1968.

Darbyshire, Lydia. *The Collector's Encyclopedia of Dolls and Toys*. Secaucus, NJ: Chartwell Books, Inc., 1990.

Doll Collectors of America, Inc. *Doll Collectors Manuals*, 1942, 1946, 1949, 1956-57, 1957, 1973. Self-published.

_____. *Doll Collectors Manual*, 1983. Cumberland, MD: Hobby House Press, Inc., 1980.

Doyle, Marian I. An *Illustrated History of Hairstyles, 1830-1930*. Atglen, PA: Schiffer Publishing Ltd., 2003.

Enkelmann, Hans Walter. Letters to the author. March 25, 2004, April 19, 2004 and June 25, 2004.

Fawcett, Clara Hallard. Dolls, *A Guide for Collectors*.

New York: H.L. Lindquist Publications, 1947.

_____. Dolls, *A New Guide for Collectors*. Boston, MA: Charles, T. Branford Co., 1964.

Foulke, Jan. *Blue Books of Dolls and Values*. (1st through 16th editions) Cumberland and Grantsville, MD: Hobby House Press, Inc., 1974-2003.

_____. *Doll Classics*. Cumberland, MD: Hobby house Press, Inc., 1987.

_____. *Focusing on Dolls*. Cumberland, MD: Hobby House Press, Inc., 1988.

_____. *Insider's Guide to China Doll Collecting*. Grantsville, MD: Hobby House Press, Inc., 1995.

_____. *Kestner, King of Dollmakers*. Cumberland, MD: Hobby House Press, 1982.

_____. *Simon & Halbig Dolls, The Artful Aspect*. Cumberland, MD: Hobby House Press, Inc., 1984.

Fraser, Antonia. *Dolls*. London: Octopus Books Limited, 1963.

_____. *A History of Toys*. Frankfurt, Germany: Delacorte Press, 1966.

Goodfellow, Caroline G. *Understanding Dolls*. Woodbridge, Suffolk, England: Antique Collectors' Club, 1983.

_____. *The Ultimate Doll Book*. New York: Dorling Kindersley, Inc., 1993.

Hart, Luella. "Marks Found on German Dolls and Their Identification." *Spinning Wheel's Complete Book of Dolls*. New York: Galahad Books, 1949-1975.

Hillier, Mary. *Dolls and Doll Makers*. New York: G.M. Putnam's Sons, 1968.

Johl, Janet Pagter. *More About Dolls*. New York: H. L. Lindquist Publications, 1946.

_____. *Still More About Dolls*. New York: H.L. Lindquist Publications, 1941.

_____. *The Fascinating Story of Dolls*. New York: H.L. Lindquist Publications, 1941.

_____. *Your Dolls and Mine, A Collectors' Handbook*. New York: H.L. Lindquist Publications, 1952.

King, Constance Eileen. *The Collector's History of Dolls*. New York: St. Martin's Press, 1978.

Mackay, James. *Childhood Antiques*. New York: Taplinger Publishing Co., 1976.

MacDowell, Robert and Karin. *The Collector's Digest of German Character Dolls*. Cumberland, MD: Hobby House Press, Inc., 1981.

Mathes, Ruth E. and Robert C. *Toys and Childhood, The Mathes Collection and Philosophy*. Cumberland, MD: Hobby House Press, Inc., 1987.

Matheson, Marie. "Dating Parian Dolls." *Spinning Wheel's Complete Book of Dolls*. New York: Galahad Books, 1949-1975.

Merrill, Madeline O. *The Art of Dolls 1700-1940*. Cumberland, MD: Hobby House Press, Inc., 1985.

_____ and Perkins, Nellie. *Handbook of Collectible Dolls, Volume II*. Saugus, MA: Self published. Printed by Woodward and Miller, Inc., 1969.

Mueller, Marion Christiana. *Reise ins Spielzeugland*. Erfurt, Germany: VHT Verlaghaus Thüringen, 1997.

Noble, John. *A Treasury of Beautiful Dolls*. New York: Hawthorne Books, Inc., 1971.

_____. *Dolls*. Toronto: The Ryerson Press, 1967.

Ray, Marcia. *Collectible Ceramics, An Encyclopedia of Pottery and Porcelain for the American Collector*. New York: Crown Publishers, Inc., 1974.

Richter, Lydia. *China, Parian & Bisque German Dolls*. Grantsville, MD: Hobby House Press, Inc., 1993.

Roentgen, Robert E. *Marks on German, Bohemian and Austrian Porcelain, 1710 to the Present*. Atglen, PA: Schiffer Publishing Ltd., 1997.

Sandon, John. *Antique Porcelain*. Woodbridge, Suffolk, England: Antique Collectors' Club, Inc., 1997.

_____. *Collecting Porcelain*. Great Britain: Octopus Publishing, Inc., 2002.

_____. *Starting to Collect Antique Porcelain*. Woodbridge, Suffolk, England: Antique Collectors' Club, 1997.

Scherf, Helmut. *Thüringer Porcelain*. Leuchtenburg Museum, 1978.

_____. *Thüringer Porcelain*. Wiesbaden, West Germany: Ebeling, 1980.

_____, Klauss, Hans; Koch, Ursula: Pohl, Karin and Wendle, Anke and Martin. *On the Porcelain Road*. Rudolstadt, Germany: Rudolstadter Heimathefte, 1995.

Singleton, Esther. *Dolls*. Washington, DC: Hobby House Press Inc., 1927.

Smith, Patricia. *China and Parian Dolls, Identification and Value Guide*. Paducah, KY: Collector Books, 1979.

_____. *German Dolls, Featuring Character Children & Babies*. Paducah, KY: Collector Books, 1979.

_____. *Kestner and Simon & Halbig Dolls, 1804-1930*. Paducah, KY: Collector Books, 1979.

St. George, Eleanor. *Dolls of Three Centuries*. New York: M. Barrows & Co., Inc., 1951.

_____. *Old Dolls*. New York: M Barrows & Co., Inc., 1950.

_____. *The Dolls of Yesterday*. New York: Bonanza Books, 1948.

Tarnowska, Maree. *Rare Character Dolls*. Cumberland, MD: Hobby House Press, Inc., 1987.

Tessmer, Angelika. *Sonneberger Geschichten*. Hilburghausen, Germany: Verlag Frankenschwelle, 1995.

_____. *Sonneberg Geschichten, Von Puppen, Griffeln und Kuckspfeifen*. Hildburghausen, Germany: Verlag Frankenschelle, 1996.

Trimble, Alberta. *Modern Porcelain, Today's Treasures, Tomorrow's Traditions*. New York: Harper and Brothers Publishers, 1962.

Theriault, Florence. *Hertwig & Co. Archives, 1890-1937*. Annapolis, MD: Gold Horse Publishing, 2000.

Vogel, Janice and Richard. *Conta & Boehme Porcelain, Identification and Price Guide*. Ocala, FL: Self Published, 2001.

Wendl, Martin and Schafer, Ernst. *Spass am Sammeln, Altes Thüringer Porzellan*. Rudolstadt, Germany: Griefenverlag, 1984 and 1990.

White, Gwen. *A Book of Dolls*. New York: G. P. Putnam's Sons, 1966.

Whyel, Rosalie and Hedrick, Susan. *The Rose Unfolds*. Bellevue, WA: Doll Art, Inc., 1996.

Young, Helen. *The Complete Book of Doll Collecting*. New York: G. P. Putnam's Sons, 1967.

Acknowledgments

First and foremost, I would like to thank Susan Bickert and Roland Schlegel for making my four books possible. From my first tour of the A.W. Fr. Kister porcelain factory in 1999 to my dumping-ground digs at the Thuringian porcelain factories in 2003, Susan and Roland have arranged every one of my special doll research and photography days in Germany. Their encouragement and help has been invaluable.

Another very special friend who has contributed in a major way to my four books is Christiane Gräfnitz. For the past five years, Christiane has made trips to Thuringian museums to photograph unusual dolls in their collections for my books. She knows many curators of German museums, and they have allowed her to photograph dolls that are on display and also in the storage areas. Christiane has been wonderful about answering all of my doll-related questions, year after year.

Estelle Johnston has also helped me in many, many ways. She encouraged me to write this book, and has offered suggestions every time I asked for help. And, throughout my research, she has unselfishly shared her extensive knowledge of parians with me.

I am very grateful to the following doll collectors for allowing me to include his or her special doll(s) in this book: Jeppe Christensen, Kenneth Drew, Kathy and Mike Embry, Margaret Hartshorn, Estelle Johnston, Andrea Jones, Barbara Kouri, Ann Meehan, Craig Nelson, Erik Nilausen, Susan Moore, Fred Olson, Terry and Tom Schmeltzer.

I sincerely thank the following Thuringian museum curators for their permission to publish photographs of their collections in this book. Sonya Gürtler, curator of the Deutsches Spielzeugmuseum, Sonneberg, was extremely helpful during Christiane's photography sessions at the museum. She kindly let me use copies of the museum's inventory sheets to accurately date and describe each doll. She also contacted two Hertwig family members for me to secure permission to publish photographs of their original sample boards. The sample boards, currently on loan to the Sonneberg museum, are owned by Dr. Christopher Hertwig, who inherited the boards from his father Ernst Friedrich Hertwig, and Sophie Berlinger, daughter of Hans Hertwig.

I also appreciate the valuable help from Peter Cramer, curator of the Ohrdruf Town Museum in Ohrdruf; Christel Ziermann, curator of the Pössneck Town Museum in Pössneck and Thomas Reinecke, curator of the Schloss Tenneberg Museum in Waltershausen. Additionally, I would like to thank Jeppe Christensen and Erik Nilausen, owners of Olga's Fancy Museum in Copenhagen, Denmark, for allowing me to include dolls from their collection in this book.

The pictures in my book are the result of many, many hours of work by the following talented photographers: Gene Abbott; Valerie Jo Coulson of Curtis Haldy Photography; Michael D'Elia of Image Arts Etc; Pierre Dutertre of Red Kite Studios; Anne Friis; Curtis Haldy of Curtis Haldy Photography; Ann Hanat of Black Cat Images, Inc.; Margaret Hartshorn; Estelle Johnston; Andrea Jones; John Kouri; Gregg Smith and Jim Young of Digital Image, LLC.

Joy Smith of Robin Imaging Services is responsible for all the photographic laboratory work. I am very grateful for all she has done for me. Astrid Ledbetter translated many books and magazine articles for me. Her translations allow American doll collectors to learn about German doll production from original sources. I truly appreciate every hour she has spent on my behalf.

Last, but definitely not least, my whole family has offered unwavering support for my German-doll research. They have encouraged me to continue my doll-related activities year after year. My son, Lee, taught me to use a computer so that I could write my books. He continues to patiently solve all of my computer problems, large and small. And for forty-eight years my husband, Herb, has helped me every day in so many ways.

About the Author

Mary Krombholz holds a 27-inch un-tinted shoulder-head doll made by the A.W. Fr. Kister porcelain factory in Scheibe-Alsbach, Thuringia. (Photo: Kirtley Krombholz)

Mary Krombholz is the author of three previous books about antique German dolls, including *German Porcelain Dolls, 1836-2002* and *Identifying German Chinas, 1840s-1930s*. She has been writing about antique dolls for the past sixteen years. Her monthly column, "Gems of the Doll World," was published in the weekly newspaper *Antique Week* from May 1989 until May 2002, and her articles appear frequently in *Doll News* and *Antique Doll Collector*. Mary Krombholz regularly presents programs and seminars at the national annual conventions of the United Federation of Doll Clubs (UFDC) and received the UFDC Award of Merit for Educational Endeavors at the 2001 national convention in Atlanta. An accredited National Antique Doll Judge, she is serving as the UFDC Apprentice Judge Instructor for antique dolls from 2006 through 2008. She has traveled to Germany every year since 1993 to research dolls. Mary Krombholz is an economics honors graduate of the University of Maryland.